100 *Years of*
DAILY
WORD

CELEBRATING
100 YEARS
1924–2024

100 Years of DAILY WORD

Edited by ELLEN DEBENPORT

unity®
Books

100 Years of Daily Word

Bible quotations from the American Standard Version and New Revised Standard Version unless otherwise noted.

First edition 2023

Cover design: Hailee Pavey
Interior design: Laura Carl and Hailee Pavey

ISBN: 978-0-87159-427-3
Library of Congress
Catalog Card Number: 2023941909
Canada GST: R132529033

A Note
TO THE READER

Those of us in the Unity publishing department began several years ago to imagine and create this book in time for the 100th anniversary of *Daily Word*® in 2024. Some of us spent weeks in the Unity Archives reading through messages of the past century, which still speak Truth to us today. Others researched the past editors of *Daily Word* and the international growth of the magazine. Still others envisioned the design of this book.

We learned that *Daily Word* was created with the Unity Prayer Ministry, known as Silent Unity®, in mind. The inventor of *Daily Word,* Frank B. Whitney, wanted people who contacted Silent Unity for prayer to have an inspirational message they could read each day. For several decades, *Daily Word* reflected its strong ties to Silent Unity, even including monthly prayer lessons for *Daily Word* readers.

The format of the messages changed a bit over the years. You might notice different styles, especially in the early years when messages took the form of lessons. It seems odd now, but *Daily Word* was several years old before the messages became focused on a single word for each day.

The chapters in this book have been composed like the magazine itself, a combination of articles, poems, and inspirational messages. The 12 topics chosen for the messages in this book, such as healing, guidance, and so on, are those that now appear in every issue of *Daily Word*, based in part on the most frequent prayer requests that come into Silent Unity. To build each chapter, one article and two poems on the topic have been included, along with two messages on the topic from each decade.

As you read through the years, you may notice changes in the use of language and the understanding of God. For many decades, the language was masculine—God as *He* or *Father*, or *man* to mean all humanity—which was considered proper English at the time. Some of the messages describe God doing things for us, while others—especially those written more recently—emphasize our own spiritual nature and inner power.

The messages are in chronological order through each chapter, from the 1920s to the

2020s. You may want to read the book straight through. Or you might choose a topic that speaks to you on any given day and read from that chapter. You could simply let the book fall open and read the message that presents itself. The articles and poems in each chapter are not chronological but were included because they fit the topic.

Poems and articles in the early days were not always attributed to an author, but you also will see some writers' names more than once. James Dillet Freeman was an especially prolific author and poet who devoted his entire adult life to Unity. Some of the same Bible verses, too, were repeated in different messages through the years, and various translations were used. Early on, sometimes well-known authors were quoted instead of using scripture.

Our anniversary celebration would not be complete without hearing from our readers. The reader testimonials interspersed throughout these chapters are mostly recent and are used with permission. Initials are used to protect privacy, but these are real people, most of whom shared their thoughts with Unity when they were renewing their subscription or giving a subscription to a loved one. Their voices echo the readers' devotion and love for this publication that has carried *Daily Word* through its first century.

As you can imagine, so much rich material from *Daily Word* of the past could not be included in this book. So many messages of inspiration and comfort are nestled in the bound volumes of *Daily Word* that reside in the Unity Archives. You may hold these original copies and read their messages should you ever visit Unity Village. But thanks to advances in technology since 1924, you may also read a century's worth of archived messages online as part of your digital subscription. Visit *dailyword.com* for more stories and memories celebrating 100 years of *Daily Word*.

—Your Friends at *Daily Word*

Table of Contents

Chapter 1

Daily Word: THE PAST 100 YEARS

REV. TERESA BURTON, *DAILY WORD* EDITOR

From time to time I wonder what Frank B. Whitney would think of *Daily Word* if he were alive to read it today. One hundred years ago, Whitney, *Daily Word*'s creator and founding editor, launched the publication intended to be a "manual of daily studies" for Unity students and all others eager to learn and practice the principles of spiritual Truth.

To that end, Whitney, a longtime Unity employee, explained in the foreword of the inaugural issue of July 1924, "The teachings will be as absolute as is consistent in making Truth clear to minds of various degrees of spiritual unfoldment. The power of the Word will be taught day by day."

A century later, in a world that has changed in countless ways, this daily devotional from Unity remains true to that goal, even while evolving to reflect a deepening understanding of metaphysics and stretching linguistically to meet the needs of a modern readership.

A Worldwide Presence

I doubt Whitney and his contemporaries dared dream of the impact this slim devotional would achieve over the years. *Daily Word* is now translated into four languages and is read in more than 100 countries. The braille version is sent to more than 500 readers, and daily audio messages are available in English and Spanish.

An international publication with a subscriber base of approximately 400,000, *Daily Word* is a light and a hope, a beacon of singular Truth shining in an increasingly complex world. Given *Daily Word*'s reach and influence, it's awe-inspiring to consider its humble beginnings as the brainchild of a single man, serving a spiritual movement that, like him, was not yet 40 years old.

Daily Word *and Silent Unity*

Daily Word's inception can be traced to the Unity Prayer Ministry. Whitney had worked for Unity in a variety of roles, including as a letter writer for Silent Unity. Writing to those who had contacted Silent Unity for prayer, he concluded they would benefit from a daily reminder of Truth and dedicated the remaining 14 years of his life to producing *Daily Word* monthly, writing most of the messages and affirmations himself.

This link to Silent Unity would endure and deepen through the next significant editorial tenure, that of Martha Smock. Prior to the beginning of Smock's 33-year editorship, she served as an instructor in the Silent Unity letter writing department. In the style of the affirmative prayers she wrote and taught others to write, Smock described *Daily Word* this way: "It serves as a daily reminder that nothing is

> Even today, the link between *Daily Word* and the Unity Prayer Ministry continues. Each issue contains a page of affirmations used each month in the prayer ministry. Readers are invited to use those same statements of Truth in their individual prayer practice.

hopeless or impossible, and reaffirms that we are spiritual beings who can meet any situation happily, effectively, and constructively."

Even today, the link between *Daily Word* and the Unity Prayer Ministry continues. Each issue contains a page of affirmations used each month in the prayer ministry. Readers are invited to use those same statements of Truth in their individual prayer practice.

Roots and Wings

Daily Word, while remaining remarkably consistent in its format, has undergone some cosmetic changes during the decades. For instance, the earliest issues were devoid of color, photography, and graphic design elements. Today, each issue features a colorful photograph on the cover, often of a locale, animal, or natural or human-made creation. Talented graphic artists lend visual meaning to the poems and stories, and each issue is vibrant with color throughout.

Other, deeper changes pertain to the messages themselves. In *Daily Word*'s earliest years, the messages were instructional and absolute in tone, declaring metaphysical Truth, almost as a challenge to readers to take it on and live it. In those earliest messages, no mention was made of the state of the world or societal conditions. The comfort readers could find in those early words was in the absolutism of metaphysical Truth. It was almost as though the messages' subtext was: *It doesn't matter what the state of the world is. It doesn't matter what the state of your life is. Truth is Truth. Use it.*

Later writing would soften, taking a more comforting, inspirational tone. These messages would mention the transitory realities of fear, grief, and illness and provide inspiration to turn to a more enduring Truth. This sensibility would evolve even further to mention with increasing consistency that this Truth of God as the one presence and power is not only something to realize, but also something to call upon from within and to use to face human circumstances, overcome difficulties, and create the lives we wish to live.

From Newtonian Certainty to Quantum Fluidity

This development happened in tandem with growing understanding of metaphysics in Unity and beyond. At the time of the inception of *Daily Word* in the early 20th century, people worked from an understanding of Newtonian physics, meaning, among other things, that we live in a cause-and-effect universe. In this framework, it's easier to appreciate the absolutism that characterized the earliest messages. After all, the conviction that the thoughts held in an individual's consciousness would be reflected as the circumstances of that person's life left little room for consideration of contributing factors such as societal conditions or global trends.

Later, the understanding of quantum mechanics would introduce an element of unpredictability and commensurate creative freedom to the understanding of Truth. *Daily Word* messages began to reflect that. The writing expressed compassion for the human condition and inspiration for humanity's ability to rise above it using a combination of spiritual tools, including, but not limited to, the practice of Truth through affirmative prayer.

Free and Unlimited

Today we're continuing to move the messages in a bold, new direction. Our writing declares—with increasing consistency—that the power and presence of God is not just *in* you—it *is* you. We're not surprised that this is not a comfortable direction of growth for some readers. Many report feeling bereft, wondering where God has gone. The answer is simple if not altogether easy: God is where God has always been, expressing as the light in each mind and the love in every heart. We pray these messages help you deepen in spiritual understanding and access the power and strength that are among your divine gifts.

As Our Second Century Begins

It is a joy to share the Truth of God and the Truth of you as a spiritual being. May *Daily Word* messages and stories continue to bless, comfort, and inspire you and lead you to realize you are fully, gloriously divine and endowed with the ability to live the Truth you know.

Rev. Teresa Burton became the editor of *Daily Word* in 2019.

The Making of
DAILY WORD

The Making of
DAILY WORD

After a century of publication, it would be impossible to count or name all the writers, editors, designers, and printers who have been involved in the creation of *Daily Word*. We can be grateful to each of them for the role they played in bringing spiritual inspiration to millions of people—often at exactly the times they needed it.

Looking back, a few of the people and processes stand out. In this section you will read about the creator of *Daily Word* and two of its longest-tenured editors, as well as the global growth of *Daily Word* and how the magazine is transformed from ideas at Unity Village to the printed pages in your hands.

Daily Word *Editors*

What does an editor do? In the case of *Daily Word*, the editor works with a team of daily message writers—people scattered across the U.S., some of them Unity ministers and some not—first assigning words for each to write about, then making sure the messages flow smoothly and fit onto each page of the pocket-size magazine. The editor also finds writers to share uplifting stories and an inspirational poem in each issue. Overall, the editor makes sure the magazine reflects the spiritual teachings of Unity and shapes each issue to speak with the voice of *Daily Word*.

Interestingly, in a full century there have been just 10 editors for *Daily Word*, some holding the position for decades. For them, it has been a calling and a ministry, not just a job.

HERE IS A ROSTER OF EDITORS IN THE FIRST 100 YEARS OF *DAILY WORD*:

Frank B. Whitney: Editor July 1924 to September 1938. Whitney is considered the founder of *Daily Word*. See the profile of Whitney in the following pages.

Bernice Minter: Editor 1939 to 1944.

Martha Smock: Editor for 33 years from 1944 to 1957 and then again from 1964 through 1984. See profile in the following pages.

Billie Freeman: Editor 1957 to 1964.

Jeanne Allen: Editor 1984 to 1985.

Colleen Zuck: Editor 1985 to 2009. See profile in the following pages.

Laura Harvey: Editor 2009 to 2014. In 2009, *Daily Word* became a bimonthly magazine with two months of messages in each issue.

Beth Hammock: Editor 2014 to 2015.

Elaine Meyer: Editor 2016 to 2018.

Rev. Teresa Burton: Began working as editor in May 2019. Because of lead times for the magazine, her name first appeared in the January/February 2020 edition.

Frank B. Whitney's Divine Idea

By Ellen Debenport

Although his name may not be familiar today, Frank B. Whitney was the creator, founder, and first editor of *Daily Word*. He is best remembered for one divine idea: that people seeking support from the Unity Prayer Ministry, known as Silent Unity, would appreciate an uplifting message to begin every day. He suggested a little booklet of devotionals to be sold by subscription.

It's interesting to note that *Daily Word*, which became the flagship publication of Unity, was not the brainchild of Unity founders Charles and Myrtle Fillmore. But they surely supported Whitney's idea. Beginning with the first issue on July 1, 1924, Whitney wrote nearly all the messages and many of the poems in *Unity Daily Word* for the first 14 years of its existence, until his death in 1938. The name was shortened to *Daily Word* in 1937.

Whitney's obituary in *The Kansas City Star* recalled, "The editor carried into his writings and work for the Unity School of Christianity a natural buoyancy and optimism."

Born in Kansas in 1889—the year Unity was founded—Whitney practiced as a dentist for four years before he came to work at Silent Unity in 1915. Three years later, he became dean of the Unity Correspondence School, which had been established by Charles Fillmore to teach students outside the Kansas City area, sending one lesson at a time with student assignments returned by mail. The Fillmores considered Unity to be a school rather than a church.

"These lessons will give every student a training in the demonstration of prosperity, as well as health, and with each lesson he will manifest the teaching in health, harmony, and understanding," the Fillmores told *Unity* magazine in 1909.

Whitney led the correspondence school from 1918 to 1924 until he began *Daily Word*. Lessons by mail continued until 1973 when more students were able to travel to Unity Village for study.

Unity Village was nothing but open land when Whitney started *Daily Word*. Unity headquarters was operating in downtown Kansas City, Missouri, and "the farm" was a weekend getaway for employees. It would be a few more years before the Tower and Silent Unity Building were dedicated at what became Unity Village—now an incorporated town with 1,200 acres.

While he was editor of *Daily Word*, Whitney wrote four books for Unity: *Creed of the Dauntless* (1930), *Open Doors* (1932), *Mightier Than Circumstance* (1935), and *Beginning Again* (1938). His writing also was included in *Be of Good Courage* (1953) and the hymnal *Wings of Song* (1984).

After his first year at Silent Unity, Whitney in 1916 married a young woman just out of high school, Clara May Hoagland, who the same year succeeded Myrtle Fillmore as director of Silent Unity. Better remembered by her second husband's name, May Rowland went on to lead Silent Unity for 55 years.

Rev. Ellen Debenport is vice president of publishing for Unity World Headquarters.

First-Ever Daily Word *Message*

After Frank B. Whitney got the go-ahead to begin publishing a magazine of daily devotionals, he began with this:

JULY 1, 1924

God in me is my light and my understanding.

"God, who commanded the light to shine out of darkness, hath shined in our hearts, to give the light of knowledge." (A.V.) "The earth shall be full of the knowledge of Jehovah."

"The truth that God is the Father of man does away with the oft-proclaimed presumption that it is impossible for the finite to understand the Infinite." —*Christian Healing*, Charles Fillmore

In order to have spiritual understanding, man must first realize that he has capacity for it. When one acknowledges that it is natural and right for man to have full knowledge of the Infinite, he is but confirming his own ability to enjoy infinite understanding. Man is the manifestation of God within, and, in His likeness, is all-wise and all-knowing.

To believe in the real presence of God as Divine Mind in you is to identify yourself with all light and knowledge. Man is primarily mind and is necessarily unlimited mentality. He takes his God-given dominion and power first through consciousness, and, consequently, must have full possession of all truth.

Begin today to rise out of the belief that by nature you are limited in understanding. Never think or say that anything is too difficult for you to comprehend. Think at all times of man as capable of knowing all truth. Learn to rely upon the light of God within to make clear whatever you wish to know.

Martha Smock Still Inspires

By Mallory Herrmann

Martha Smock's legacy in Unity extends well beyond her 33 years of service as editor of *Daily Word*. Having grown up in the Unity tradition, she helped share a message of hope and faith with readers worldwide—young and old, religious and agnostic—reminding them of the truth about themselves.

Smock's family was steeped in the Unity tradition. When Smock was born in 1913, her mother sent a birth announcement to her friend Myrtle Fillmore, who had founded Unity with her husband Charles in 1889. Smock was raised in Unity, attending its Sunday school and even spending time with the Fillmores.

> She was a frequent contributor of daily messages and helped the magazine grow to more than 2.5 million subscribers by the time of her passing.

When Smock married her husband Carl in 1935, the officiant was Rev. Ernest Wilson, the internationally renowned author and speaker who was editor-in-chief of Unity publications at the time.

A Leap of Faith

In 1930, as the Great Depression was wreaking havoc on families nationwide, Smock had just graduated from high school at 16 and was living with her family in Kansas City. She and her sister Ruth applied for work with Sears to support their household, but only Ruth was hired. Smock would say later it was divine order that she ended up working at Unity instead, first in the files and then as a letter writer and instructor in the Silent Unity prayer ministry. She later assisted Frank B. Whitney, who had founded a magazine of prayer messages called *Daily Word*.

In 1944, May Rowland suggested that Smock take over the role of *Daily Word* editor.

Smock, just 30, wasn't sure she was ready for the position, but Rowland had no doubts. Rowland had been a young woman herself when she was appointed director of Silent Unity in 1916, and she had complete faith in Smock's capacity to edit the beloved booklet.

Smock went on to serve as editor from 1944 to 1957 and again from 1964 to 1984. The break came when her family moved to Long Island, New York, but they found their way back to Kansas City—and Unity Village—just a few years later. Billie Freeman, who served as *Daily Word* editor in the interim, told Smock she'd only been keeping the chair warm for her.

As editor, Smock sometimes worked from home—a unique situation at the time—using paper files and a typewriter. When she was working on campus at Unity Village, Smock occupied the office previously used by Myrtle Fillmore herself. Just down the hall was writer and poet James Dillet Freeman in an office that had been used by Charles Fillmore. Smock and Freeman had met during their time working in Silent Unity and became quite close friends. Her daughter Kathy asked Freeman to officiate at her wedding ceremony in 1971, for which he wrote his now-treasured poem, "Blessing for a Marriage."

The name Martha Smock didn't appear on the masthead of *Daily Word* until 1978 because, as she explained, "We try to keep personalities out of the magazine and concentrate on the message." She was a frequent contributor of daily messages and helped the magazine grow to more than 2.5 million subscribers by the time of her passing.

She also published several books, including *Meet It With Faith* and *Fear Not*, which is still in print. She was a favorite speaker at events and retreats, both at Unity Village and across the country.

Smock was given an honorary ordination as a Unity minister in 1980. Although she never took any formal classes, her daughters Stephanie and Kathy said almost no one knew more about Unity.

Smock made her transition on July 5, 1984, leaving a long legacy of faith and devotion for those who knew her personally, for the broader Unity movement, and for the millions of readers around the world who still look to the wisdom of *Daily Word* today.

Mallory Herrmann is a writer and editor based in Grandview, Missouri. A version of this article first appeared in a blessing booklet, *Messages We Need to Hear: From the Writings of Martha Smock* in 2021.

Colleen Zuck: Artist to Editor

By Mallory Herrmann

Colleen Zuck's tenure as *Daily Word* editor stretched nearly a quarter of a century. In that time, she made herself at home with both the people and the teachings of Unity.

While her biggest contribution to the magazine's history was made as editor, Zuck got her start on the design side as a keyline artist. She had already been working as a keyline artist at National Bellas Hess, a North Kansas City mail-order house, when she was first introduced to Unity. A friend, whose father was a manager in the printing shop at Unity, recommended Zuck for a new position there, and before long she had a new job.

Zuck got her start in the publishing department in 1969, preparing camera-ready book and magazine copy and art for publishing. She was soon promoted to the graphic arts department and, after honing her writing skills, was promoted to assistant editor and later editor of *Wee Wisdom*®, the Unity magazine for children.

Finding a Calling

She quickly realized that becoming a part of the Unity community was all in divine order. She was meeting new people, learning about spiritual principles, and pursuing an unexpected career path.

"People could see something in me that I couldn't see for myself," she said in an interview. And because Unity has a history of investing in its own people, it was an opportunity Zuck couldn't miss.

Zuck was editor of *Wee Wisdom* for eight years—bringing stories, poems, games, and beautiful artwork to children all over the world. Then in 1985 she was appointed editor for *Daily Word*, where she oversaw the publication of the magazine, including the Spanish version,

La Palabra Diaria. She served as the *Daily Word* editor until her retirement in 2009 and was at the helm when the magazine celebrated its 75th anniversary in 1999. "Golly, it's awesome to see *Daily Word* now celebrating its centennial!" she said.

Throughout her tenure, she knew she wasn't in it alone—especially when facing the usual publishing challenges of managing timelines and meeting deadlines. She credits the tremendous support she received from those around her.

"I was able to do what I needed to do because I knew it wasn't about me being the editor," she said. "It has never been about one person or one editor. Editors have changed over time, but *Daily Word* has remained a steady source of inspiration for generation after generation of readers."

One Message, One Community

Over the years, Zuck had opportunities to interview a wide range of subjects including some prominent names of the time, like comedian Phyllis Diller and broadcaster Robin Roberts. She also fondly recalls interactions with Unity figures over the years, especially when James Dillet Freeman, beloved Unity poet and minister, would deliver the poems he wrote

> [Zuck] quickly realized that becoming a part of the Unity community was all in divine order.

for *Daily Word* by hand. He infamously didn't ride the elevators, but instead walked up three flights of stairs to turn in his poem and share some stories about his life in Unity with Zuck.

"It really speaks to the unity among people," she said, noting how important a shared sense of community and purpose is. "Division is destructive, but through *Daily Word* there is an opportunity to continue spreading the Truth and the message of the power for good that's within each person."

She fell in love with how accepting and embracing the Unity community—and the *Daily Word* audience—is. "*Daily Word* still shares the same positive message, translated and shared all around the world, coming from a friend who is always affirming the best about each and every person as a creation of God."

Mallory Herrmann is a writer and editor based in Grandview, Missouri.

Daily Word *International*

By Lois Cheatham

Unity doesn't have missionaries—or does it?

In the early years of Unity, Truth students traveled abroad to share Unity principles and pamphlets. American troops carried copies of *Daily Word* and Unity pamphlets while serving on foreign soil. Their sharing of a simple yet meaningful little magazine stirred interest and brought comfort during unsettling times. Much of the work abroad began with these individuals.

Today's "missionaries" are called "affiliates" who volunteer their time and use their own resources to reprint and distribute *Daily Word*. Unity provides a digital file containing the magazine's articles and daily messages, then affiliates have it printed and mailed to their subscribers.

At various times, *Daily Word* has been translated into Afrikaans, Chinese, Dutch, French, Russian, and Tamil. Because affiliates are self-supporting, their ability to translate and produce a magazine can change. On its 100th anniversary, the magazine is being distributed in English, German, Portuguese, and Spanish, reaching more than 100 countries.

Unity had already started translating some of its publications into Spanish when *Daily Word* was created in 1924, but it was three decades before the magazine was translated as *La Palabra Diaria*. It is still translated at Unity Village and circulated to Spanish-speaking readers, many of them in the United States as well as other countries. Rev. Carmen Fe Figueroa in the Dominican Republic leads a robust outreach for *La Palabra Diaria*, hosting weekly radio and television programs where she shares some of the messages.

In the case of the German and Portuguese editions, volunteers translate the magazine and produce it for distribution. These devoted individuals make sure subscribers have ready access to daily inspiration. However, the methods they have for sharing *Daily Word* vary.

More than 20 years ago, Rev. Anthony Habib in Trinidad and Tobago felt *Daily Word* should be readily available to everyone. He began offering the magazines in dress shops, bakeries, bookstores, movie theaters, grocery stores, and more. The magazines were placed in a decorated little box with a slot for payment. Offered on the honor system, it's reported that there was always more money in the box than expected from the sale of the magazines. This method of distributing *Daily Word* continues today in Trinidad and Tobago.

Rev. Daniel Fisher in Guyana worked for a power company by day while overseeing the printing and distribution of *Daily Word* in his time off. He also served as the director of Silent Unity in Guyana. He maintained a "Unity" phone in his work office (with the approval of his supervisor) and beside his bed so he would always be available to answer calls, whether for the magazine or for prayer support. I remember being on a call with Fisher when his special "Unity" phone rang beside him. Fisher tucked the receiver with my call under his leg as he took the other call. Upon returning, he apologized, saying calls on the other phone were confidential—a sacred trust maintained by Silent Unity throughout the world.

Following the devastating earthquake of 2010 in Haiti, Rev. Yves Lafontant, former director of *La Parole Quotidienne*, the French edition of *Daily Word*, teamed with Revs. Figueroa and Sarah Sanchez to help create an undated version of *Daily Word*. Without dates attached, its messages could be read anywhere, anytime. Select messages were chosen to support current circumstances in Haiti. Lafontant translated the messages into French in a matter of days. Transport in and out of Haiti was limited to emergency services only, so Figueroa and Sanchez stepped up to get the magazine printed and hand-carried over the Dominican Republic border into Haiti, where it was distributed by a group of volunteers.

On its 100th anniversary, the magazine is being distributed in English, German, Portuguese, and Spanish, reaching more than 100 countries.

Rev. Beatriz Bell and her husband Frank produced a version of this same undated magazine in Spanish. They worked through emergency services organizations to distribute it in regions of Argentina where devastating mud slides and other natural disasters had occurred. (Their story is later in this book.)

Rev. Lourdes Alvarez-Collado in Venezuela and a team of volunteers ride the city buses handing out free copies of *La Palabra Diaria*. The messages of hope and inspiration encourage many facing economic challenges.

Rev. Valerie Freckleton in Jamaica took to the streets to hand out copies of *Daily Word* and pray with those in bars and poor areas of town. Because of her work, she was asked to lead a meeting between rival gang members.

During the Covid pandemic, while supply and mail systems were halted in many countries, affiliates relied on the internet to get the daily messages to subscribers, sometimes meeting online or sharing the messages in emails. Not even a pandemic could interrupt the affiliates' service to others.

The powerful messages tucked inside the 80 pages we know as the bimonthly *Daily Word* have encompassed our world through the dedication of volunteer affiliates and other ordinary people who share the messages in unique ways and during unusual circumstances. Truly, *Daily Word* has traveled throughout the world on the wings of love.

Lois Cheatham worked nearly 40 years at Unity World Headquarters and served as the program manager for International Services and Outreach.

Daily Word *and Message of Hope*

By Rev. Mark Fuss

Message of Hope®, the department at Unity responsible for distributing *Daily Word* to those in need, has been touching hearts and changing lives for more than 130 years.

The Unity Free Literature Fund was initiated in April 1890 by Charles Fillmore, just a year after he and wife Myrtle founded Unity. Twenty years later, Fillmore was inspired by a verse in Luke: *"The Lord appointed seventy others and sent them on ahead ... to every town and place where he himself intended to go (Luke 10:1)."* Fillmore renamed the free literature program Silent-70.

Led in its early days by Kate Robinson and Nina Wright, and championed by Unity luminaries such as Lowell Fillmore and Imelda Octavia Shanklin, Silent-70 was often referred to as the missionary department at Unity. Thousands of publications were sent each month to readers who joined Silent-70, "scattered throughout the world, each doing a share in the bringing of eternal life and happiness into the lives of all of those about" (*Unity* magazine, April 1914).

One member reported, "The tracts and books have all been received, and already I have given out several to persons whom I know will enjoy reading them. And I hope they will be benefited by them as I have been, spiritually, mentally, and physically. My stomach is well. I am entirely free from the pain and am feeling better than I have for a year" (*Unity* magazine, April 1914).

In 1924, the newest Unity publication, *Daily Word*, quickly became the magazine at the forefront of the free literature ministry. Its daily inspiration struck a chord and became a lifeline for many in need.

In 1935, Unity began publishing *Daily Word* in braille. This continues today with Unity offering free spiritual resources in accessible formats for those with visual impairments. About 900 subscribers receive *Daily Word* and Unity materials in braille or on audio CD each year.

Through the years, *Daily Word* has provided a vital outreach ministry in prisons and correctional facilities, army camps, YMCA organizations, and merchant marine libraries. A 1951 *YOU [Youth of Unity] Magazine* reported: "The American Merchant Marine libraries are located in 15 different seaports in the United States, and Silent-70 has been sending books and periodicals to all these libraries for many years. The publications are eagerly read by thousands of men who sail our merchant ships, those who keep watch on our lonely lighthouses and lightships, and those who man the vessels and stations of the U.S. Coast Guard."

A former Silent-70 manager, Carol Riead, wrote about the importance of *Daily Word* in Unity outreach in the *Fall 1996 Progress Newsletter*. "*Daily Word* may seem small and unpretentious—but it is powerful. Every time we share a *Daily Word* magazine with someone who is in a hospital, in prison, or in other difficult circumstances, we provide an opportunity for Spirit to change a life from despair to hope and from sadness to the joy of God's love."

In 2003, the Silent-70 department was renamed Message of Hope and the program became part of the outreach department at Unity.

Today, Unity Outreach and Message of Hope distribute a variety of spiritual resources in English and Spanish, including print and digital booklets, audio recordings, and more to individuals and communities that need them most.

More than 400 Unity and New Thought churches and 900 other organizations, including hospitals and hospices, are given materials of spiritual support through Message of Hope. In turn, tens of thousands of individuals are blessed by this program each year. A hospital chaplain in Texas wrote to us: "Publications that are available in Spanish are priceless. Our program of spiritual care is more inclusive thanks to Unity."

Daily Word still leads the way, with 25,000 annual subscriptions and many thousands of individual copies distributed free of charge to those in need. As it has been since 1890, this program is entirely supported by generous donations and love offerings from those whose lives have been blessed by *Daily Word* and other Unity materials.

In recent years, 75,000 copies of a timeless *Daily Word* were printed and distributed through the gift of a generous donor. Without dates on each page, it can be used anytime, any year. This undated version of *Daily Word* has made its way into prisons, hospitals, hospices, unemployment offices, and so many places where its inspiration is sorely needed.

If you would like to support the outreach of *Daily Word* and Message of Hope, visit *unity.org /messageofhope*.

Rev. Mark Fuss is vice president of Outreach and Engagement at Unity World Headquarters.

Putting It in Print

By Martin Fisher

Growing up, *Daily Word* was always on the coffee table in our family room or at our breakfast table. Someone in our family was reading it most every day, sometimes aloud, sometimes in quiet reflection. When I graduated from college and moved to Minneapolis, Minnesota, I got my own subscription.

These days, I sometimes read *Daily Word* in the morning for several days in a row. Other times, it sits on my coffee table for several days, then I read six or seven daily messages all in one meditation session. Sometimes I refer to the word calendar and turn to the message that speaks directly to what I'm interested in at that moment. In whatever way the month unfolds, *Daily Word* is my spiritual companion and teacher—sometimes reminding me of spiritual Truths I already know but have temporarily forgotten, other times opening my mind to new ideas for growth. *Daily Word* helps me stay "prayed up," to remain continuously conscious of Truth principles and how I can apply them in my daily living—an important practice taught by our brother and Way Shower, Jesus.

My family has run a high-volume printing and mailing company since 1958. My father started the business from scratch. I worked in the business when I was a kid and began working with my dad full time after I graduated from college. When my father passed away in 1985, I bought the business from his estate, and that's been my primary business focus ever since.

After my father passed, I gave a great deal of thought to the higher purpose of the business: What should we be striving for in the years ahead and how could we best serve humanity, our associates, and clients? Creating a good place for our associates to work, helping clients grow and build on their missions, earning a profit—all good, but it seemed as if the higher purpose for the existence of our business should be much more.

As I personally strive each day to be a perfect expression of the goodness of God, I came to understand the higher purpose for our business is to do the same: to serve God and be a perfect expression of all the goodness of God for the benefit of humankind, our associates, clients, and community. God expresses through the activities of, and operations of, our businesses. This is my ongoing prayer for our businesses.

My family attended a Unity church all my life, and I became a supporter of Unity Village, visiting for retreats at least yearly. When then-CEO Tom Zender learned I was involved in publishing and direct mail, he asked whether I would like to see the *Daily Word* operation and took me on an impromptu tour of the Unity publishing department. In those days, *Daily Word* was printed at a commercial printer in Kansas City, Missouri, and printed sheets were delivered to the Unity publishing department. Unity then folded the sheets, bound the magazine, and mailed it from Unity Village to hundreds of thousands of subscribers.

Always mindful of the importance of being good stewards of its funds, Unity was evaluating the most cost-effective way to produce *Daily Word* in the 21st century. After a careful study, it was determined that it would be more efficient to use a commercial printer for all facets of the operation. Unity put out a request for proposals, and our Fisher Group ultimately won the high honor of serving as the printer and mailer of the magazine. I was truly thrilled and continue to be so today. I felt this was a dream come true because our family would be playing a meaningful role in supporting a ministry that is so important to so many people in the world. I feel the opportunity to serve Unity supports my intention for the higher purpose of our organization: to serve God and humankind and to be a perfect expression of all the goodness of God.

When we are in production with *Daily Word,* I love to walk through our plant and watch the pages coming off the presses, bringing the beautiful photographs and spiritual Truth messages to life and to the world. I love to watch the pages being bound into finished magazines, then inserted in envelopes, inkjet addressed, and put in the mail stream. It really is a beautiful thing!

Everyone who works on *Daily Word* magazine does so with such care and commitment. The writers, editors, graphic artists, circulation associates, and our team members in printing and mailing each realize the significance of the ministry that is *Daily Word.* While I am indeed grateful for all of our clients, I am honored and truly grateful for the opportunity to play our role in supporting the *Daily Word* ministry.

Martin Fisher owned his printing and mailing business in Cedar Rapids, Iowa, for 43 years and now has shifted his focus to commercial real estate. At this writing, he also serves on the board of directors for Unity World Headquarters.

Messages of
HEALING

Messages of HEALING

In a sense, every *Daily Word* message is about healing, and every reader brings hope for healing to the page each day. Readers may have a desire to cure a physical or mental ailment, but at an even deeper level, they seek inner peace, guidance through troubled times, inspiration to persevere, or reassurance about the abundance of the universe. Change for the better requires a shift in consciousness, and these messages are a daily reminder of the power to improve our experience.

Healing has been a regular topic in *Daily Word* since the beginning. Some of the messages that follow, which were curated from 100 years of *Daily Word* messages, specifically address the healing of physical conditions. All of them emphasize our spiritual nature and the healing power of divine life within us.

Angels at My Side

By June Allyson

MAY 1999

Striding through Pennsylvania Station in New York City, I was a teenager full of purpose and feeling very grown up. People were staring at me and smiling, and I smiled back, sensing they somehow knew I was on my way to Hollywood to become a big star. Or, I surmised, "They must recognize me from having seen me in the smash hit *Best Foot Forward* on Broadway."

As I put *my* foot forward to board the train, however, reality hit: I was wearing my big, pink, fuzzy bedroom slippers instead of shoes. I had left my only pair of shoes back in my vacated apartment. What a sight I must have presented to those sophisticated New Yorkers!

I was off to Hollywood—shoeless, but full of hope for the future. My future had not always seemed so bright, however. My father left home when I was six months old, so my mother and I moved in with my grandmother, who became the center of my life. In her arms, I felt shielded and protected from harm. She was my guardian angel. When she died, I held in my pain, barely daring to breathe. Her tenderness toward me was the first glimpse I had of a selfless, unconditional love. In her absence, my security was gone, or so I thought.

More Angels Appear

Less than a year later, life got even harder. A severe storm with high winds and heavy rains roared through the New York area. I remember watching it quite literally with my nose pressed against the windowpane, mesmerized by the storm's fury. When it passed, I grabbed my bike, called to my dog, and headed out to see what havoc the storm had caused.

As I passed beneath a big, old, decaying tree, I heard a sickening crack. I turned just in time to see the tree coming straight at me. I had no time to run, and the falling tree hit me squarely, breaking half the bones in my body and killing my puppy.

My mother and I were already living in abject poverty, and now it was questionable whether I would survive such massive injuries. However, God had a plan, which included angels already in place to help me. My doctor had a wonderful, loving manner and inspired me to *want* to live. The nurses hovered over my small body, helping me to find comfortable positions.

As I lay in my hospital bed, I dreamed of recovering and becoming a doctor. I was so touched by the tenderness and love being given to me that I wanted to be able to share this healing love with others. And even though the doctor and the nurses were cheering my every move, no one believed that I would ever walk again, much less become a doctor. Not even me.

However, Marie Spinosa, a swimming instructor, heard about my injuries and volunteered to devote her entire summer to my recovery. I was overwhelmed by such a selfless act of mercy, and her belief in me infused me with hope.

"What is lost can be recovered," Miss Spinosa would tell me daily as she guided me around in the pool, slowly rebuilding my atrophied muscles and limbering up my reluctant limbs. On days that I felt well enough to venture out, some of my friends from school would push my wheelchair to the local movie house, and I would sit for hours, watching Ginger Rogers/Fred Astaire pictures. As I sat in the darkened theater, another dream began to fill my heart.

I promised God that if I were able to walk again, I would not only walk, I would dance. I would earn enough as an entertainer to get my mother and me out of poverty and, hopefully, bring happiness to others. Big promises for such a little girl, but I was certain that God would send more earthly angels to help me.

A Promise Come True

Because of Miss Spinosa's unrelenting guidance, I began to recover. Soon I was out of the wheelchair and on to crutches. Finally I advanced to using a brace. I worked up enough courage to experiment with dancing—haltingly at first because I was hampered by the brace. Once I was back in school, I told my girlfriends that I could dance—as well as Ginger and Fred. Skeptics one and all, they showed me a newspaper notice, announcing auditions for a new Broadway musical. Ignorance is bliss, believe me. I didn't even know what an audition was! So when one of my friends bet me a quarter that I was too scared to go, I said, "What's the address?"

Most of the girls at the audition were taller, older, and vastly more sophisticated than I. Naturally they were—I was only in seventh grade! When the piano player asked for my music, I said, "What music?" I finally came up with the name of a popular tune of the day. Miraculously, I was asked to return the following day.

At the callback, I was in the middle of the same song, actually in midword, when a voice cut in from the dark in front of the stage. "No, no, hold it!" The man continued, "Please, please, we've got to hire her, because if we don't, she'll come back and sing that song again and again, and I can't stand it!" There was a huge laugh at the end of his little speech, for the voice belonged to Richard Rogers, who had written the song. So I got the job, won the quarter, and found a way to keep my promise to God.

Throughout my life—during my career at MGM; my wonderful marriage to actor Dick Powell, which included our precious children, Pam and Richard; my blessed marriage to Dr. David Ashrow after Dick's death; and my favorite role as grandmother to grandson Rickie—the spirit of God has been with me. God has guided my life and career with a loving hand and continued to send angels when I needed them most. I know that what my husband Dick said to me many times is true: "Junie, God is love."

Yes, Dick, you were so very right. God *is* love, and I thank God for filling my life with loving people who have been angels at my side.

June Allyson is a multifaceted actress, singer, and dancer of stage, screen, and television. Her career has included 23 films and many appearances on television, including her own show, *The DuPont Show with June Allyson*. June is actively involved in charity work for the June Allyson Foundation and works as an advocate for senior issues. [Update: June Allyson, who often played the "perfect wife" in movies with Jimmy Stewart, Van Johnson, and others, died in 2006 at age 88.]

Affirmation

Elizabeth Searle Lamb

I affirm my health
with faith,
with assurance,
with enthusiasm.

I affirm my wealth
with expectation,
with joy,
with exuberance.

I affirm my life
with love,
with rejoicing,
with a knowing
of my perfect oneness
with God.

I have faith in the healing power of God in me.

JULY 12, 1924

Daily Word's *first-ever healing message*

We all can see our bodies with the "single eye" of which Jesus spoke, and, through this faith in the reality of the invisible body, regenerate the flesh.—*Christian Healing* [Charles Fillmore]

Jesus knew the truth about the body so well that he did not behold disease as reality. Those who keep disease in mind, when they declare health, are double-minded. The ideal body is in the mind's eye. When we cease thinking of disease, the physical body is regenerated through the action of the inner body consciousness. We then manifest a perfect body like the perfect body in the ideal.

Keep piling up faith. Eventually your faith in the regenerating power of God in you will overbalance the faith that you have had in your personal beliefs in physical limitation and disease. The invisible body is to the body consciousness a tangible thing. It lives. You will be compelled to acknowledge and accept it if you are loyal to the truth and see that nothing but health can be true.

Faith is fidelity to Principle. Be faithful to truth and to the power of your word. Give no credence to beliefs that anything, save the regenerating, revitalizing presence of God, can give you health.

"It was neither herb, nor mollifying plaster, that restored them to health: but thy word, O Lord, which healeth all things." (Apocrypha)

"The prayer of faith shall save him that is sick."

Through unity with my indwelling God,
I am lifted up and healed.

NOVEMBER 30, 1925

All healing methods, whether applied to self or to others, consist in making a unity between the individual and the universal Consciousness.—*Christian Healing* [Charles Fillmore]

In order to be healed, one must consciously relate himself to the Healer. He must turn from faith in external things and make contact with his indwelling God. In this way he lays hold of abundant life and health at its very source.

Much of the failure to demonstrate health comes from inability to contact God. Whether one is giving a metaphysical treatment for himself or another makes no difference; both must be based upon the healing life and power of the divine in the individual.

When one touches the spring of healing within himself, this health flows out to the very circumference of his being. He is exalted and healed. He is lifted to a higher consciousness of himself, and healing results. The Christ consciousness has manifested itself as perfect man.

Healing methods which suppose that any power other than God can heal are temporary and unsatisfactory because they are not based upon that which is eternal. The temporary relief received from external remedies often leaves one in a worse condition than he was in at first.

"The power of the Lord was with him to heal."

The healing presence of God in the midst of me quickens, purifies, heals, and strengthens me.

AUGUST 20, 1932

The healing presence of God in your midst is mighty to lift you out of all belief in disease and weakness. When you have realized your oneness with this presence, you cannot experience disease. This presence is the presence of your own perfect health.

If you would be healed, you must take your thought off disease. You must cease to think of disease as having reality or being in Truth. You must know that only the wholeness and perfection of God, your own wholeness and perfection, is true. In this way, you will cease to feed the disease thought which has been outpicturing itself in your body. You will come to know health as your divine right and birthright.

Turn from the belief in disease and weakness, and realize the trueness of your strength, perfection, and health. Give the health thought an opportunity to express itself in your physical organism. Be loyal to God by believing in His perfection and wholeness, manifesting in and through you.

Behold, I will bring it health and cure,
and I will cure them.—Jeremiah 33:6

45

Steadfastly proclaiming my unity with the risen Christ, I am quickened and healed.

MARCH 20, 1939

You are steadily going forward in the glory and light of the risen Christ. This light is healing. It searches out your divinity and reveals your unity with Jesus Christ and His unfailing healing power.

His healing power is radiant with His Spirit of eternal life and wholeness. It penetrates darkened minds and they comprehend His perfect life and peace. It enters into curtained eyes and they see. It opens closed ears, strengthens and renews the faltering heart. It rests upon those who seek healing and they are restored to perfect vitality and health.

Steadfast faith accomplishes certain and lasting results. Let him who is in a high state of consciousness not descend into the distractions of doubt and fear. Let him be steadfast. He who has been lifted up and glorified as the all-powerful Son of God has drawn you to Himself. His healing power is doing its mighty work through you now.

That I may know him, and the power of his resurrection.
—Philippians 3:10

I am quickened in spiritual consciousness,
and I am healed in mind, body, and soul.

JUNE 8, 1943

Spiritual healing is that which comes to our physical body when the mind and soul have been healed. It comes through first putting out of mind all unholy thoughts and thinking on the life, health, love, goodness, mercy, righteousness, and power of Spirit. We cannot think simultaneously of perfection and imperfection. Either one thought or the other must have first place in our mind.

As we think only from the standpoint of Truth, we are quickened in spiritual consciousness and our healing comes swiftly. As we are regenerated in mind and soul, disease and pain lose their power over us and disappear from our body.

We know when we have experienced a spiritual healing, for we feel a distinct change in mind and soul, and then our body is healed. We know that we have been lifted to the Christ and that He has done His quickening, redeeming, regenerating work in our threefold being.

Then shall thy light break forth as the morning,
and thy healing shall spring forth speedily.—Isaiah 58:8

God in the midst of me is mighty
to bless and to heal me.

AUGUST 7, 1945

Affirmative prayer is the most effective form of healing prayer because it recognizes and accepts the truth that the healing work of Spirit is constantly going on. The prayer of supplication implies doubt, whereas the prayer of affirmation expresses faith, and faith is the most important requisite for healing.

The healing work of Spirit is constantly going on in the body, because life is present throughout the organism, and it is the nature of life to renew itself, to rebuild, to restore. Wherever life is present, the restorative powers of life are at work. These restorative powers are accelerated when man's thought is in harmony with them. The affirmative prayer establishes this harmony and makes man's consciousness an open channel for the healing work of Spirit.

Affirm: *God in the midst of me is mighty to bless and to heal me.* Know that even as you speak the words God's healing work is being done in you.

The prayer of faith shall save him that is sick.—James 5:15

From the Readers of Daily Word

Daily Word *has provided me with inspiration since I was a teenager. Everyone would benefit from reading its words of God's love and guidance.*

—B.J., NEW YORK

Reading Daily Word *is an uplifting spiritual blessing that makes me realize how fortunate life can be when we focus on the beauty, peace, and joy the writers' words bring to a person's soul.*

—E.M., FLORIDA

I think Daily Word *has helped me cope with all my life situations—thank you!*

—V.J., KANSAS CITY, MISSOURI

I have faith in God's healing, loving care.

OCTOBER 12, 1955

When we in Silent Unity pray for healing for those whose needs are brought to our attention, we give thanks that the persons for whom we pray not only are quickened with the life and power of God, but that whatever they need in the way of comfort, help, or expert care is given them.

Today we ask you to join us in praying for healing. If you are in need of healing, include yourself in the healing thought; if you have a dear one in need of healing, include him in the healing thought. Also let your love and prayers reach out to include all the unseen and unknown friends who are looking to Silent Unity for help today, who may be reading this lesson at this very moment.

As you join us in giving your special thought and blessing today to those who need healing, a great prayer of faith will go forth, a great surge of spiritual power will be felt, and miracles of healing will be wrought.

The prayer of faith shall save him that is sick,
and the Lord shall raise him up.—James 5:15

I accept my healing now.

APRIL 30, 1959

The first step in any healing is a willingness to accept healing. When some inharmonious condition has been of long duration, we tend to feel helpless about it. The man at the pool of Bethesda thought his inability to enter the healing waters at a special time prevented his being cured. Jesus showed him that healing depends purely on the receptivity of man to the perfect will of God. "Wouldest thou be made whole?" Jesus questioned.

The man had been infirm for such a length of time that he found it difficult to accept the idea of wholeness for himself. But Jesus' command, "Arise, take up thy bed and walk," swept away the false belief, and the man was healed.

Today I accept my healing, utterly, joyously, completely. I know that nothing can come between me and God's freeing, healing love. I am immersed completely in the radiant life of God. All that is not perfect is swept away. In the radiance of God's living presence I am strengthened and I am made whole.

I accept my healing now.

Wouldest thou be made whole?—John 5:6

I hold to the idea of healing life.

AUGUST 29, 1963

When someone near and dear to us needs healing, how do we react? With fear? With anxiety? Or do we hold fearlessly, confidently, calmly to the idea of God's healing life, filling him, flowing through him, healing and renewing him?

Every time we think of someone who needs healing, this can be our thought, this can be our prayer, this can be our faith: "God's life is in you, strong and powerful and healing. His love surrounds and enfolds you. His peace fills, soothes, sustains, and comforts you. His power upholds and strengthens you." As we hold to the idea of healing, we shall be praying effectively and imparting healing life through our prayers.

We find that we have to take our stand continually for life, for healing. We cannot be cast down by negative reports. We cannot allow ourselves to go along with depressing thoughts. Our reaction, our expectation can remain positive and powerful as we stay with the idea of healing life, proclaim life, believe in life, have faith in life.

The prayer of faith shall save him that is sick,
and the Lord shall raise him up.—James 5:15

> *I can be healed, for God is the healing*
> *power in the midst of me.*

OCTOBER 2, 1968

I can be healed. This is a most important realization in the overcoming of any condition. This is the first step toward healing—simply to know, to believe with all my heart, "I can be healed." This is a starting place; this is firm ground on which to stand; this is a statement of faith. "I can be healed."

I hold to this idea; I let it be in my mind, in my heart, a constant source of reassurance. "I can be healed." With God all things are possible; with Him there are no conditions impossible to heal. I can be healed, for God is the healing power in the midst of me. His life is my life. My body is His holy temple, and His healing stream of life flows in and through me. I can be healed.

If I am praying for someone else who needs healing, whenever I think of him, I affirm silently, "You can be healed." I hold to this Truth; I stay with this idea. "You can be healed." God is the healing power in us. God is the life in the midst of us.

We can be healed.

With God all things are possible.—Matthew 19:26

Courage

Grenville Kleiser

Press on! Though mists obscure
The steep and rugged way
And clouds of doubt beset,
Soon dawns the brighter day.

Keep on! Though hours be long
And days deep-fraught with woe,
Let patience have her perfect work
And vanquish every foe.

Hope on! Though all seems lost
And storms beat high,
Have faith! Be still and know
That God is nigh.

I believe in healing, I pray for healing, and I expect healing.

JUNE 24, 1972

In the book *Meet It with Faith*, we read, "All healing is spiritual; all healing comes from God. Jesus emphasized again and again that our part in healing is faith, belief, and receptivity." If we are praying for healing, let us pray first for increased faith. Let us remember that all healing comes from God. All permanent healing comes from within, for it is a healing of the inner man, a healing of the soul as well as of the body. Healing is more than relief from physical pain or ills. It is the result of cooperation with the natural action of God-life within.

It does not matter what the appearance is or what some condition is diagnosed to be, there is only one life, the life of God, and that life is in us right now. Let us be still and acknowledge God's presence of life and healing power at work in us. Let us affirm for ourselves or others: "I believe in healing, I pray for healing, and I expect healing, for God is our life, strength, and wholeness."

And the prayer of faith will save the sick.—James 5:15

I give thanks that there is a healing power upon which we may rely. I go my way rejoicing.

NOVEMBER 13, 1973

It is not easy to stand by when someone near and dear to us is experiencing a serious health challenge. We long to be able to do something to help. At such times we can find peace of mind and assurance in the realization that there is a great healing power upon which we may rely. No matter what the appearance or condition or seriousness of the need, God is the one healing power. He is the healing power mighty in the midst of the one for whom we are praying. Upon this we can rely.

To rely upon God's healing power is another way of saying that we have faith. Faith is the assurance that God's love and power are present and unfailing. So when we rely upon God's power to heal and to restore a dear one, we are praying in faith.

When we rely upon God's healing power, our prayers are more powerful, for they are then affirmative prayers, they are prayers that produce results, they are prayers that call forth healing.

The power of the Lord was with him to heal.—Luke 5:17

I have faith that all things are possible,
that I can be healed.

JULY 2, 1980

My body has a marvelous capacity to throw off disease, to heal itself. This is because I was created out of God-life. This life is the very substance of my being; healing power is present within me.

Faith, that positive quality of thought and feeling in me that trusts absolutely in God as the healing power, brings healing. Everything in me responds to my faith.

Affirmations of Truth and life, affirmations that remind me that I am a spiritual being, that my body is the temple of the living God, increase my faith. Such affirmations have a powerful and positive effect on my body.

My body listens to my words—the words I speak aloud, the words I speak to myself. Words of life and healing revive a spirit of healing in me and help to establish in me the strong faith that all things are possible, that I can be healed.

Faith cometh by hearing, and hearing by the word of God.
—Romans 10:17

I rejoice! Complete healing is a reality in my life because I am created for life.

APRIL 20, 1988

Jesus did not discriminate in the healings He performed. He did *not* say that some could be healed, but that others could not be healed. Jesus healed all who came to Him for healing. The healing power that Jesus evoked was the healing power of God, and this healing power is present today just as it was in the time of Jesus.

There is no condition that cannot be overcome. I hold to this conviction. I believe it. I affirm it. I know that the more I hold to the spiritual idea of health, the stronger I become in faith. The more I affirm the idea of health, the more quickly I am made a channel for the healing power of God, either for myself or for another.

The healing power of God in the midst of every person accomplishes the healing. I rejoice in the realization that everything in me and in those for whom I pray tends toward healing, because we are created for life.

It is the spirit that gives life.—John 6:63

In mind, body, and heart, I am open and receptive to the healing life of God.

FEBRUARY 23, 1994

The healing life of God is aglow in every atom of my mind and body.

I remain in a steady flow of the healing activity of God as I give it my undivided attention. I think about the purity of God-life within me. I praise God for unlimited healing possibilities. I relax in the healing life of God and feel its warm glow soothing me through and through.

I live and move in the healing life of God, and divine life lives and moves in me. Several times a day, I think about the wonder of life in me and give thanks for it.

Throughout the day, I acknowledge the presence of God's renewing activity. As I do, I enter into the joy of health, wholeness, strength, and vitality. All I have to do to receive it is to be open in mind, body, and heart to God's healing life.

Enter into the joy of your master.—Matthew 25:21

The life of God is moving through me to strengthen, heal, and restore me.

SEPTEMBER 14, 1998

For 12 years a woman had endured much and had undergone many different treatments without even a glimmer of healing. Still she had faith, and with that faith, she reached out to touch Jesus' cloak. What elation she must have felt at being healed!

When I am praying for my own or another's healing, I remember not to give up hope. I understand that the inner healing which is taking place may not always be visible. Still, I have faith.

I feel a peace that can only contribute to my healing and convey a tangible hope to others for their healing. The relief I feel soothes me and invites a healing flow to move through me.

My faith reaches out to embrace others with a belief in their complete healing.

He said to her, "Daughter, your faith has made you well; go in peace, and be healed of your disease."—Mark 5:34

From the Readers of Daily Word

I read it every day. I apply it to how I try to live. Thank you for this inspiring booklet every day.

—D.F., NEW JERSEY

I couldn't live without my Daily Word.

—G.P., MARYLAND

Thank you always for this wonderful and supportive guide in my daily life.

—L.P., NEW YORK

The spirit of God is healing and renewing me now.

JUNE 13, 2000

Meditating on the renewing life of God within me is a healing therapy that I can apply every day. So I find a quiet, comfortable place to sit, close my eyes, and relax.

Allowing an inner vision to play on the screen of my mind, I recognize that a healing is taking place within my body. Healing energy is moving through every organ and muscle, every joint and bone. Pain is eased, and all anxiety ceases.

As I breathe deeply, my lungs fill with life-sustaining oxygen. I am invigorated and the surface of my skin tingles with renewal. I hold to this vision of healing for a few moments more, knowing that healing is my reality. The spirit of God is healing and renewing me now.

On the glorious splendor of your majesty, and on your wondrous works, I will meditate.—Psalm 145:5

I am strengthened, prospered, and made whole.

MAY 17, 2006

I may have a very specific, focused outcome in mind as I pray for a healing. In actuality, my healing may take place in a different or broader form than I had anticipated. God's healings come in many forms, arrangements, and timings.

As I pray for healing, I make and allow room for God's perfect work in my life. I trust God's power to heal whatever needs to be healed. Even if this healing is something other than what I had had in mind, I know it is for my best. I am prepared to receive a healing in whatever form it comes to me.

I thank God for healing and renewing me. With faith in God, I am strengthened, prospered, and made whole.

And by faith in his name, his name itself has made this man strong, whom you see and know; and the faith that is through Jesus has given him this perfect health in the presence of all of you.—Acts 3:16

I am renewed by the healing power of God.

APRIL 18, 2011

Spring rains bring relief from the harshness of winter. Under their gentle caress, the earth returns to its lushness, the fog of winter is washed away, and signs of new life appear.

My time in meditation is like the healing rains of spring. As I open my heart to the grace of God, I am renewed. In God's loving presence, I feel restored. My fears dissolve, my needs are met, and my soul is refreshed. Hope, health, and well-being blossom within me.

The healing power of God is eternal. Though darkness may at times seem to obscure it, the quiet of prayer washes away any doubt. The life of God enlivens my being. I am whole and well.

It will be a healing for your flesh and a refreshment for your body.—Proverbs 3:8

I accept the healing that is mine.

DECEMBER 4, 2019

I understand that I am a spiritual being who is living a human experience. When I begin to internalize and fully live this truth, I discover that in Spirit I am whole and well in body and mind.

However, in my present consciousness I may be experiencing illness in the form of a health challenge or perhaps as the result of a past trauma or past relationships. I see this moment as a divine opportunity to transform, to heal, to grow, and to learn from challenges I am facing.

I know that as a spiritual being I am perfect but not yet perfected; I am whole yet still healing. I accept this opportunity as a gift from God, a way for me to accelerate my spiritual growth. With gratitude, I continue my healing journey.

He said to him, "Do you want to be made well?"—John 5:6

I celebrate wellness as my healing is revealed.

FEBRUARY 22, 2022

Healing, the realization of wholeness, is a natural process. I do not need to control or coerce my healing, but I do need to cooperate with the divine pattern of wholeness within me. As I do, restorative energy flows through my entire being.

I aid my healing with positive thoughts and expectations and with peaceful interludes communing with God in prayer. I regularly give thanks for the infinite intelligence informing my body and mind.

I also assist my healing by caring for my physical, mental, emotional, and spiritual needs. I eat well and engage in uplifting conversations. My prayers and affirmations of faith, along with my commitment to healthy living help me know my wholeness.

Then your light shall break forth like the dawn,
and your healing shall spring up quickly.—Isaiah 58:8

Messages of
FAITH

Messages of FAITH

When *Daily Word* readers seek spiritual support, they often are endeavoring to renew or bolster their faith. They know they are never outside the presence of God. They know their good is already available if not yet visible. They know faith the size of a mustard seed can move mountains. Faith is remembering and believing Truth when facing what seems to be evidence to the contrary. For 100 years, *Daily Word* has helped readers recover and strengthen their experience of faith in any circumstance.

Some Questions Answered

A Q&A with May Rowland

JULY 1969

One of the most popular features of the 1968 Unity Village Vacation Retreats was the appearance of May Rowland at the healing-prayer workshops. May Rowland, Director of Silent Unity, shared the platform with Foster McClellan of the Department of World Unity, who, as moderator, presented questions to her which came from the retreatants in the audience. This program was completely spontaneous and was so well-received that we felt we should share some of the answers to questions that concern people everywhere.

May Rowland is uniquely qualified to answer these questions. For many years she has directed the Silent Unity healing-prayer ministry where prayer is continuous around the clock. Charles and Myrtle Fillmore began this work [in 1890], and through the years people from all over the world have written, telephoned, or wired for prayer help and healing counsel. May Rowland says about Silent Unity, "This is an eternal work; I work under the direction of Jesus Christ, and will go on forever."

Tell us about prayer, May Rowland.

Prayer is the practice of the presence of God. Prayer is not just something we fall back on in some time of great need. In Unity we use affirmative prayer. Some persons ask how we can say, "This situation is not real," about a broken arm, for instance. We don't say it is not real, but we say it is a condition that needs to be changed. We recognize the spiritual nature. We are not just a body with a pain, but essentially a spiritual being.

Relaxation and prayer work are important. Silence, the inner realization of God's presence, has to be practiced. Keep practicing.

Eventually you will feel that you have touched the presence of God. The purpose of the silence is to contact the Spirit within you. God is present within you. God is omnipresent, but you contact His presence at the center of your being. Say to yourself, "Be still." Relax. Practice being quiet. Relax. Let go. Feel the presence.

When you say, "Our Father," and praying the Lord's Prayer, instead of thinking of God as being way out there somewhere, know that you are contacting the Lord of your own being within you.

Keep in mind that the Christ center is within and work from the center. In praying, remember that you are not praying to God outside you. God is everywhere, but you contact Him within.

We expect to eat three meals a day. Prayer is just as important. Spiritual ideas are spiritual food. Prayer consciousness is imperative till every thought is lined up with it. Some persons ask how long they should pray. It is not a matter of time; the consciousness of prayer is continual …

Prayer should become a habit, something that is constant. We can pray while driving a car, washing dishes, whatever we are doing, wherever we are. We develop a prayer consciousness, not just when there is a great need, but all the time we practice living in the very presence of God.

How can one find what one is really meant to do in life after the children are grown and one is left all alone?

Take this thought, "I resolve to let the will of God be done in my life and affairs." Think of what you want and put it into words, into positive form. Resolve to let the perfect will of God work through you, and have the courage to follow the inspiration that comes.

What is meant when we say that man is a spiritual being?

The Spirit in us transcends our personal self. We need to think of the transcendent power in us. What we put into our consciousness is important. We can identify ourselves with that which is less than we are; or we can identify ourselves with the truth about us, which is that we are spiritual beings. A helpful affirmation to remember is, "I transcend myself and all my affairs, for I am Spirit."

Why is a person very kind and loving and then the next moment very cruel and spiteful?

Many people act this way. Rather than getting upset, it is best to overlook it, and not to judge by appearances. We should always pray for the other person. And our prayer should always be for his illumination. As we pray for illumination for others and also for ourselves, we will try to understand what makes another person act the way he does. As we hold to the idea of the constructive, harmonizing, unifying power of love, we will be blessed and we will be a blessing. Really, this is a healing need; if we think of it in this way, we will not be upset and we will be able to be of help through our loving prayer ...

How do you train yourself to pray more deeply?

- ◆ You can start with the *Daily Word*.
- ◆ Let prayer become a part of your life.
- ◆ Put affirmative prayers into your mind.
- ◆ Meet in mental agreement with Truth ideas.
- ◆ Practice the presence of God.
- ◆ Concentrate. Train the mind.
- ◆ Repetition and agreement are both needed.

[May Rowland succeeded Myrtle Fillmore as director of Silent Unity in 1916 and served 55 years until her retirement in 1971. In 1916, she married Frank B. Whitney, the founder and first editor of *Daily Word*, and she was a frequent contributor to the magazine all her life.]

From What a Small Seed

James Dillet Freeman

From what a small seed grows
so great a tree!

Dear God, there is such a
small seed in me,

There is in me a hunger and a need

To put down roots of faith that I
may feed

Upon the unseen rivers of Your love,

A never-ceasing urge to reach above

Myself, to put on spiritual height,

To grow up straight and

lithe into Your light.

How tall are redwoods!
But what is the span

Of Spirit? the dimensions of a man

Made in your likeness?
To that I must aspire,

Must always go down deeper,
come up higher,

Till I am anchored in You,
You my ground

And You the light with which
my life is crowned.

I have faith in God, in myself,
and in my fellow man.

DECEMBER 3, 1927

Without faith we would be without power to hold tenaciously to principle. Faith gives us the ability to hold firmly to God. Through faith we cling to our declarations of truth until they cause the things we seek to come into manifestation.

When one lacks faith, he cannot take a firm grip on life. He is unable to take hold of those deep and mystic forces which have power to relate to him the finer things of life.

Through faith in good, faith in divine principle, we exercise loyalty and fidelity to God. By having faith in the power and existence of good we cause it to manifest in us and in our affairs.

Faith in oneself, if rightly understood, is really faith in God. If one has faith in the higher principle and higher consciousness within him, then his faith in God is unmistakable. On the other hand, if one has faith in God and knows that God is within him, then he likewise has faith in himself.

When we recognize the spiritual nature of others and learn to see God within them, then we have faith in them. The student of practical Christianity must have faith in his fellow man.

According to your faith be it done unto you.—Matthew 9:29

My supreme faith in God, in myself, and in my fellow man exalts me above every doubtful and distrustful belief. I have unwavering faith.

OCTOBER 24, 1929

What would the world be without faith? What would your life become without faith in God, in yourself, and in others? Living without faith would be hard to contemplate. Yet there are many who find difficulty in rising out of doubt, suspicion, unbelief, and distrust.

How the world will be transformed when all persons everywhere have given up faith in the power of evil and disbelief in God! That transformation is taking place rapidly, because even the most hardened doubters are yielding to Truth.

If you should happen to be one who believes that the world is becoming worse, try to reverse your thought. Instead of having faith in the powers of darkness, behold the light of Truth now dawning in the minds and hearts of men everywhere. Decrease the seeming power of evil by increasing your faith in God. If in doubt, always give good the benefit of your wavering belief. God, the good, is sure to win out in any seeming war between good and evil.

Great is thy faith: be it done unto thee even as thou wilt.—Matthew 15:28

My faith in God, the good, in the midst of me, wipes out every trace of doubt or unbelief. I have faith.

OCTOBER 2, 1932

Faith in God, the good, relieves us from doubt. Believing in God, we cease to believe in evil, sin, disease, and failure. Our faith in God must be undivided. When we believe in the power of good, we cease to believe in the so-called power of evil.

No one is without faith in something. A person has faith in God or else he believes in the power of adversity. He has faith in God as his health or else he believes that, in some way, God produces ill health. He has faith in God as the power that causes him to be prosperous and successful or else he thinks that God, in some fashion, could bring about a condition of lack and failure.

Do you want to increase your faith? Do you want to have faith in God to the exclusion of doubt and unbelief? Then think often of God, the good. Cease to think of evil, fear, disease, and failure, and, above all, cease to have faith in their alleged power. To have faith in God you must not believe in any opposite of Him.

Your faith in the good will increase as you continue to think of the good to the exclusion of all else.

Great is thy faith: be it done unto thee even as thou wilt.
—Matthew 15:28

Through faith in God my life is transformed.

OCTOBER 11, 1939

You may think that you are lacking in faith; you may waver at times in your expression of faith; yet deep within you there is an abiding faith in God that cannot be shaken by outer circumstances or appearances. It is impossible for you not to have faith, for through faith you live. Every moment in which you live and think and move you are testifying to your faith.

In Hebrews we read, "Faith is assurance of things hoped for, a conviction of things not seen." Your faith in God assures you of unity with His life, substance, and power. Even as He has implanted in you the desire for understanding, for peace, for health, for happiness, and for plenty, so has He blessed you with the faith necessary to the fulfillment of these desires. The manner of life you live and the extent of your overcoming measure the extent to which you use your faith with understanding.

Today take a step toward remaking your life mentally, spiritually, and physically by reaffirming your faith in God.

The righteous shall live by his faith.—Habakkuk 2:4

The spirit of the living God increases our faith.

SEPTEMBER 16, 1942

Faith is a divine faculty of the mind that is ceaselessly active. It is the tool by which we shape our life and all that comes into it. According as we develop and increase our faith we grow in spiritual stature and more perfectly demonstrate the spiritual powers that our Father has given to us.

On one occasion Jesus' apostles said to Him, "Increase our faith." Jesus' response to this petition is noteworthy. He neither granted nor denied the petition. He reminded the apostles of the tremendous potential power their faith would have if they would but call it into activity. Then Jesus subtly pointed out that it is vain for us to expect our faith to do great things for us except as we begin to put it to work now.

The moment we put our faith to work the Spirit of the living God within us increases our faith so that it is always greater than any demand that we can make upon it. The more we use it the stronger it becomes.

Whosoever ... shall believe that what he saith cometh to pass; he shall have it.—Mark 11:23

I prove the power of God in my own life by my faith.

NOVEMBER 17, 1949

Today I test my own faith in the power of God. I try my faith; I use it. I begin with something small. If I have lost an article I say, with all the faith I have: "Nothing is lost in Spirit. What is mine will be returned to me. Father, I thank You that it is done now." And I go about my business knowing in faith that all is well.

If I seem to have a cold or a headache or a sore toe, I pray with faith: "Father, I now manifest Your perfection in my body, for I am Your perfect child. I thank You that I go forth whole." And I know that God's perfect will is constantly manifesting itself as perfection in my body.

If I have some small lack, I pray with faith: "Father, You already know my need. You have already produced whatever is needed to fill the lack. I open my hands now to receive in joy and thanksgiving." I am serene and sure, filled with faith that all is well.

I test my faith; I prove in my own life the power of God.

Try your own selves, whether ye are in the faith;
prove your own selves.—2 Corinthians 13:5

From the Readers of Daily Word

Daily Word *is a part of my daily habit. It helps me start my day right and when I miss a day, I miss my daily dose and feel "off." Thankfully I can come back home to get reconnected and get back on track.*

—D.A., LOS ANGELES

Love, love the Daily Word!! *Couldn't get out of bed in the morning if I didn't have my* Daily Word *to start my day!*

—G.C., AUSTIN, TEXAS

Through faith I am victorious in all things,
over all things.

MARCH 3, 1951

One of our favorite Unity songs is "Faith Is the Victory." This has been the keynote of the Unity work through the years. In every problem that has arisen faith has been the answer, and faith has been the victory.

In your own life when situations arise that call for utmost patience and understanding and reliance on all that you know of Truth, faith—the faith that God has planted in your heart—will carry you through to victory.

Faith is the victory over fear; faith is the victory over poverty; faith is the victory over disease; faith is the victory over injustice; faith is the victory over negation of any kind.

Let this strong idea of faith be your key thought for today. Faith is the victory. Keep it in your mind, keep it in your heart, express it in your life.

"Faith is the victory that overcomes the world." Through your faith you can be victorious in all things, over all things.

For whatsoever is begotten of God overcometh the world;
and this is the victory that hath overcome the world,
even our faith.—1 John 5:4

My faith is centered in God.
My life is filled with his good.

AUGUST 19, 1955

My faith is centered in God. Therefore, I am not discouraged if things do not seem to be going according to my plans. I affirm the presence and power of God, the good omnipotent, in my life and affairs. I give thanks from day to day, from hour to hour that I am being guided by infinite wisdom, that I am being blessed by divine love.

My faith is centered in all that God stands for. My faith is centered in love; my faith is centered in life; my faith is centered in supply; my faith is centered in joy; my faith is centered in light; my faith is centered in power.

Whenever thoughts of lack, ill health, or inharmony come into my mind, I bless them; I lift them up by affirming the one presence and the one power—God.

My faith is centered in God, my mind is centered in God. With my whole being I feel the nearness of His presence; with my whole being I praise the constancy of His good.

Therefore will we not fear, though the earth do change.
—Psalm 46:2

The eyes of my faith are directed to God.

JUNE 13, 1962

If we want to see something clearly, we open our eyes and look at it. As our body has eyes, so does our spirit. Our spirit sees with eyes of faith, and it is with these inner eyes that we perceive God. Let us open these eyes of faith and look to the good, look to God.

We open our eyes of faith through prayer. We do not always see the good with our physical eyes, but in prayer our faith sees and calls forth the good.

By directing the eyes of faith to God, we focus our attention on God as the source of the healing, happiness, and success that we desire for ourselves and others. Where there is need of healing, the eyes of faith perceive the quickening, renewing life of God in action. Where there is a need for harmony, the eyes of faith behold the love and happiness that God wills to express through us. Where there is a need for supply, our eyes of faith see the abundance of God filling every need.

Mine eyes are ever toward Jehovah; For he will pluck my feet out of the net.—Psalm 25:15

I press forward in faith and enthusiasm.

MAY 19, 1967

Whatever we seek to bring forth with great faith and enthusiasm will be made manifest to us. Faith is the vision that sees the good we desire and knows that it can be experienced, no matter what appears. Enthusiasm is the great energizer that bends every effort of mind and heart toward the achievement of our goal.

We need to press forward in faith and enthusiasm in order to realize our highest happiness. God has given us these two great tools of mind and heart—faith and enthusiasm—with which we can carve out of our experiences new opportunities to serve and new ways to bring creative activity into our daily routine.

As we use our faith we gain the clear vision of the good that underlies every experience in life. By linking our faith with the aliveness of enthusiasm, our good comes forth. Faith knows that the good is present; enthusiasm stirs us into action. As we press forward in faith and enthusiasm, we enjoy increasing success in all that we do.

But it is good to be zealously affected always
in a good thing.—Galatians 4:18

About Remembering

Mildred N. Hoyer

Remember those times when somebody vowed
Something could not be done?
But one with faith had tackled the task
And faith versus doubt had won?

How good to remember when challenges come,
That "within" is the place of Power;
Here prayer begets faith and here it is
Full faith comes into flower.

How good to remember this basic truth:
Faith in God will always prevail;
The future is safely in God's hands,
God's purpose cannot fail.

God loves me. I express love to someone today.

FEBRUARY 10, 1973

The intense light of faith is within me this day. All darkness disappears and I easily surmount all obstacles.

Tagore, the well-known Indian poet, gives us one of the most beautiful definitions of faith ever put into words. He writes: "Faith is the bird that feels the light and sings when the dawn is still dark."

Although everything around us may be dark, intuitively we can sense a great reservoir of light in the deep recesses of mind. It is then revealed that no amount of darkness can ever oppose this rising sun of faith. Faith penetrates all realms of thought and makes us know that all things are possible. In this state of awareness, all doubts disappear as vapor before the sun.

The greatest discovery we can ever make is that we have the Christ Mind in us, and in this discovery we find that we do have tremendous faith. The intense light of faith is within us this day and we easily surmount all obstacles that would otherwise obstruct our path.

Now faith is the assurance of things hoped for,
the conviction of things not seen.—Hebrews 11:1

Faith fills my heart, uplifts my spirit,
and invites God's goodness into my life.

APRIL 28, 1978

Faith can fill us so completely that we are faithful and faith-filled and radiant with the beauty and power of our faith. We do not need words to convey our faith. When we have faith, that faith is felt.

There is an assurance and a strength in faith. Faith makes its presence felt in a serenity of spirit. Faith fills our hearts, uplifts our spirit, and invites God's goodness into our life.

The earth moves forward in time on faith. The rising of the sun, the movement of the moon, the ebb and flow of the tides are evidence of a higher power at work.

We proclaim our faith simply by living as though we have faith. We proclaim our faith by trusting in God, by trusting in His love, by trusting in the goodness of His creation and the goodness of His people. In this steadfast trust, we are faith-filled, we are strong.

Looking to Jesus the pioneer and perfecter of our faith.
—Hebrews 12:2

My faith is strong and unwavering.
Nothing is impossible.

NOVEMBER 14, 1984

What I have faith in affects every area of my life. Where do I place my faith? Do I place my faith in persons, in things, in procedures? Do I have faith only in the tangible or do I have faith in the unseen but sure evidence of God's presence and power at work in all that appears?

I walk by faith; I live by faith; I triumph over ill health, lack, inharmony, negation of any kind through faith. In all circumstances and conditions, I take my stand in faith. I affirm my faith. I have faith in God; there is nothing to fear. I have faith in myself; I can do and be all things. I have faith in the right outworking of all the affairs of my life, for God is with me and God never fails. I have faith in the goodness of people and feel my oneness with them. My faith is strong and unwavering. Nothing is impossible.

By faith we understand that the world was created by the word of God, so that which is seen was made out of things which do not appear.—Hebrews 11:3

With unwavering faith, I affirm life,
strength, and wholeness.

DECEMBER 2, 1988

Jesus healed people who were experiencing all kinds of symptoms. He healed some conditions that had been present since birth or were considered to be incurable.

What did Jesus require of a person seeking healing? Faith! He healed a child with epilepsy after His disciples had tried without results. When they asked Jesus why they could not heal the child, He replied, "Because of your little faith. For truly, I say to you, if you have faith as a grain of mustard seed ... nothing will be impossible to you."

Faith in God as life and power sets into motion mighty currents of healing life in and through us, making us whole and strong.

Our faith steadily increases as we nourish it with living words of Truth. As we keep thinking about God's life in us and as we keep affirming wholeness, strength, and perfection, we are using faith to build a consciousness of enduring health.

Your faith has made you well.—Mark 5:34

I am true to my spiritual convictions:
my faith in God and in the goodness of God.

NOVEMBER 1, 1991

God is everywhere present and all good. Therefore, through our faith in God, we know that good can be found in everyone and everything.

However, when we are confronted with appearances to the contrary, our faith may waver. It may be years later before we recognize the good that was present, the good that our active faith can perceive at any time.

Whatever comes to our attention today in our conversations with others or in reading or listening to the news, let us determine to remain true to our faith in God, to our belief that good is in all and will be victorious.

The more we use our faith faculty to perceive the good, the stronger our faith becomes. We have unshakable and invincible faith in God, the good.

But let him ask in faith, with no doubting,
for he who doubts is like a wave of the sea that
is driven and tossed by the wind.—James 1:6

I have faith in God.

OCTOBER 13, 1999

If I ever doubt that I have enough faith to meet some challenge or to accomplish a goal, I remember what Jesus taught about faith. He shared the truth that faith—even faith the size of a tiny mustard seed—has the power to move a mountain of challenges out of the way.

I have faith in God. I trust God to show me what to do when obstacles appear in my way and to give me the strength to overcome whatever I need to overcome.

Reinforced with faith, I make great discoveries. I spend less time worrying and more time interacting with the people who are important to me. I am at ease, so I truly enjoy the companionship of family and friends.

Most important of all, my faith inspires me to take time with God in prayer every day.

If you had faith the size of a mustard seed, you could say to this mulberry tree, "Be uprooted and planted in the sea," and it would obey you.—Luke 17:6

From the Readers of Daily Word

Unity has been in our family since an American soldier gave my grandma his Daily Word *in 1945. Since then this "heart-centered metaphysics" has been the center of our faith. I myself always try, both as an artist and in my Catholic lay services and radio devotions for NDR and Deutschlandfunk, to pass on these deep truths.*

—S.C., GERMANY

Daily Word *is in my Survival Kit. It keeps my focused on a positive direction.*

—C.J-R., DETROIT

I have faith that the spirit of God
is expressing greatness through me.

JUNE 11, 2000

I have met with obstacles as I have traveled the road of life. Keeping the faith, I have overcome doubt. Looking back, I now recognize that even during those times when I was in doubt, I was not questioning the power of God. Rather, I was questioning my confidence in myself.

Experiencing what God can accomplish through me and observing what God can accomplish through others increase my faith. Faith continues to build me up spiritually, physically, and emotionally.

I have faith in God to guide me, to love me, to keep me safe. My faith is founded in the power and greatness of God.

Out of a growing faith in God, a new "me" has emerged—one that is confident and serene. The spirit of God within me is expressing greatness through me.

Out of the believer's heart shall flow
rivers of living water.—John 7:38

My faith in God carries me safely past any challenge.

APRIL 19, 2004

There are times in life that we simply could not move forward without faith. It is a bridge that spans the space between what our minds think is impossible and what with God we know is possible.

Sometimes a bridge of faith is like a simple stepping-stone in a small creek, and that is all that is needed to get past a minor challenge. At other times, when we need to cross a major river of uncertainty, our bridges of faith need to be more like steel marvels of engineering, built slowly and deliberately out of a strong trust in God and a habit of consistently applied prayer.

Whenever we pray with complete trust in God, we are building bridges of faith that encourage us and our loved ones and carry us safely past any challenge.

For I am longing to see you ... so that we may be mutually encouraged by each other's faith, both yours and mine.
—Romans 1:11-12

My faith in God sustains and uplifts me.

DECEMBER 11, 2010

From time to time, the media cover disturbing local or global events. But my faith in God need not be shaken. I know God is there for me and for all members of the human race as a constant support and guide. Whatever the situation, God is directing us to our highest good.

My faith does not depend on outward conditions. Rather, my faith is grounded in the perfection of God. With faith-filled focus, my courage and peace are unshakable, no matter the situation.

God is present in everyone and everything. I trust that right outcomes are unfolding in divine order. My faith lifts my spirits, strengthens my resolve, and fills my heart with love and expectancy.

As it is written, "The one who is righteous will live by faith."—Romans 1:17

My life demonstrates the power of my faith in God.

FEBRUARY 25, 2014

My faith in God inspires me to do more good works than I thought possible. As divine ideas come to me, I act with confidence. I express everything from simple acts of kindness to extraordinary visions of peace. I wait patiently for guidance, knowing that when the time is right, my next step will be revealed. I claim what I need and share the abundance I receive.

The good others see in my life is the flow of God's love, peace, and substance through me into the world. The secret to my good is that I live in faith. I boldly do what is mine to do. Nothing is impossible! Through faith, my success is assured.

You see that faith was active along with his works, and faith was brought to completion by the works.—James 2:22

I behold the world through the lens of faith.

MARCH 21, 2022

Living my faith does not mean seeing the world through rose-colored glasses. Instead it means taking and holding a higher view of all circumstances, in my life and in the world.

I believe in the possibility of peace, even in the midst of conflict and strife. I believe comfort is available in the presence of pain and grief. I believe healing is possible and wholeness can be realized even in a state of illness or injury.

I am fully in the world, present to its more troubling and worrisome conditions, and yet I remain untroubled in mind and light in heart. Using faith as the lens through which I view the world and my place in it, I attune myself to a greater reality. I relax into God's abundant grace, secure in my faith that all is truly well.

Now faith is the assurance of things hoped for,
the conviction of things not seen.—Hebrews 11:1

Messages of
PRAYER

Messages of
PRAYER

Daily Word was first conceived as a booklet of prayer messages for people who were contacting the Unity Prayer Ministry, called Silent Unity. For 100 years, *Daily Word* has focused on the power of prayer. Its messages have reminded readers to turn to prayer and sometimes suggested ways to practice. Alongside Silent Unity, *Daily Word* has helped readers pray through wars around the world, financial crashes, weather disasters, and sometimes shocking news stories, as well as personal ups and downs. Prayer is always available. It is the first action we take to address any situation.

The Silent Unity Prayer Team

By John A.V. Strickland

JUNE 1986

Many of us who are watching a major championship game in any sport—whether baseball, football, basketball, golf, or whatever—are seeing an illusion. We may think the championship is won on the last day of the season, in the last game of the series, or on the last hole of a tournament. The reality is, however, that the championship has been won over a period of time of preparation and training that has led to that final moment of truth.

All of us participate in championships throughout our lives, times when we prepare and train for goals that may involve education, work, health, finances, or relationships with spouses, parents, children, and friends. Life is constantly calling on us to rise to the occasion; the call is not to defeat another team or person but to be champions over our own personal challenges …

The activity of prayer prepares us for victory. Prayer conditions our minds and hearts to receive. This spiritual conditioning, like the athlete's conditioning, does not take place overnight. It is a step-by-step, thought-by-thought, feeling-by-feeling process. God is ready, willing, and able to bless us with every needed thing as soon as we have prepared our minds and hearts to receive the blessing.

When a blessing seems to be withheld, sometimes the human heart cries out in anguish, "I prayed and prayed, and still nothing happened." While this may seem to be true in the outer, in the inner something great always happens when we pray. Each sincere, faith-filled prayer does something wonderful: It helps prepare the mind and heart to receive.

For each demonstration we seek, there is a certain threshold in consciousness that we must cross. Perhaps this might be compared to a certain level of fitness an athlete must achieve to perform at his or her best. In spiritual matters, we never know how close we are to that threshold, but through faith we know that each exercise in prayer brings us closer and closer to that "championship" threshold of consciousness that we are seeking.

A word of caution here: Sometimes we pray beautiful, deeply felt, positive prayers, and then cancel them with our negative thoughts and attitudes. Each thought is a powerful thing, a kind of prayer itself. A quiet time of meditative, God-directed thought is more concentrated and more powerful than careless thoughts and words. Nevertheless, all our thoughts are powerful, formative agents—no matter how casually expressed.

As Director of Silent Unity and a former athlete, it is only natural for me to compare the prayer ministry here with that of a championship team. In Silent Unity, we pray, pray, pray. This has been going on day and night for nearly 100 years. Our training and preparation have been steady and faithful. The Silent Unity prayer team is, in my opinion, a championship team of loving, spiritually minded people. We prepare ourselves for answered prayer by praying, by being positive and faith-filled, and by speaking words of truth even when in the human sense we may not feel like it.

Prayer is continuous here at Silent Unity. A person is praying in our prayer vigil at all times. The team staffs the telephone 24 hours a day. Throughout the day, we have regular times of prayer when we meet as a group. Throughout the year we dedicate special times to the bolstering of our prayer power. These times are ones of preparation and training ...

> Each thought is a powerful thing, a kind of prayer itself.

In Silent Unity, we think of all who call or write or join us in reading *Daily Word* as special prayer partners, and as spiritual champions in life. If you have a special need, a time of facing a personal championship event, you can know that you have a highly trained, dedicated spiritual team on your side. This team is not just composed of the ... employees who work in the Silent Unity Building at Unity Village; this team is composed of the millions of praying people around the world who read *Daily Word* and who contact the Silent Unity prayer ministry by letter or telephone. With God and the continuous, faith-filled prayers of Silent Unity friends and your own spiritual training, you can meet and overcome every challenge. Always think of yourself as a Silent Unity teammate and as a champion in life. This is the truth about you. This is how we see you.

We invite you to double your prayer efforts and spiritual study this month. During this time of dedicated spiritual renewal, we offer these ideas for your upliftment: thoughts are things that you can use to change your life; prayer conditions your mind and heart to receive blessings. Championships are won through preparation, and you are a spiritual champion in life. We welcome you on the Silent Unity prayer team—a world champion one, if I do say so myself!

[Rev. John Strickland served as director of Silent Unity from 1983 to 1991, succeeding James Dillet Freeman, who had served for 50 years. He also led Unity churches in Jacksonville, Honolulu, and Atlanta before he retired.]

[To contact the Unity Prayer Ministry, also known as Silent Unity, call 816-969-2000 or go online to *unity.org/prayer*.]

Stop and Pray

[Uncredited]

When things about you are disturbed
and all the world's amiss,
When other persons seem to take
away your joy and bliss,
There's but one thing that you can do
if you would clear your day:
Cease thinking of disturbing
things—stop where you are and pray!

"Stop, look, and listen," warns the
sign at a busy thoroughfare,
And so in life this warning's good to
free you from all care.

Stop thinking all disturbing thought
and look to Christ instead,
And listen to His guiding voice if by
Him you'd be led.

And when in life you see that you
have troubled thoughts in mind,
There's but one thing for you to do if
happiness you'd find;
Stop, look, and listen—stop and pray!
Let Christ have His own way!
You'll find your troubles come to end
if you but stop and pray.

God in me answers my prayers with an abundance of his supply.

MARCH 27, 1925

If we make proper connection with Divine Mind in this kingdom of heaven within us, the Father will surely answer our prayers. No good thing will he withhold from us if we comply with the law of righteous asking. —*Christian Healing* [Charles Fillmore]

When through prayer we contact that mighty living fountain of power within us, we start the flow of abundance toward us. From this inner realm pours out the fulfillment of our most exaggerated expectations. We get the consciousness of just how to do whatever we desire to do. We see the solutions of all our problems. We see the actual demonstration and manifestation of what we desire.

Man has at the center of his being the key which unlocks universal treasuries. He has the abundance of God at his disposal. The riches of the kingdom within are at his command. The love of God pours forth as the solution to all problems on the plane of human love. The life of God pours out as the vitality and energy of man's physical body.

All must turn to God, God within the being of man, if they would have the bounty of God expressed in themselves. They must see salvation come as the saving power of God within themselves. They must turn their faces upward, not downward; within, not without.

"O thou that hearest prayer, unto thee shall all flesh come."

In the consciousness of the power of praise, I praise and increase the good that appears in my life.

AUGUST 26, 1929

In spiritual consciousness we find ourselves so happy, so full of joy, that we want to praise, to give thanks for every blessing that appears in our lives. We almost want to shout for joy at every evidence of God's love manifest in our affairs.

Those who follow the plan of praising the good sometimes think that they have made a surprising discovery. They discover that praise has the power to increase and magnify the thing upon which it is poured. They find that their good is increased through the power of praise.

Praise has power to bring out of the seeming void the very thing for which we pray. Praise seems to be a second step of prayer. After we have prayed for something our next step should be to praise and give thanks for its appearance.

Begin to praise your good. Praise your own commendable acts to yourself just as you would audibly praise another for the good that he does. Do not withhold praise at any time unless you are specifically led to do so.

Give unto them ... the garment of praise
for the spirit of heaviness.—Isaiah 61:3

> *I keep in a state of constant prayer by frequently meditating upon my oneness with God within me.*

JUNE 30, 1931

I have learned the truth that there is nothing mysterious about prayer. I have found it to be a simple process, one involving only my conscious relation with Spirit within me. In this consciousness I feel the power of prayer, the force that comes from knowing my oneness with God.

In prayer, I do not beg God or beseech Him for anything. I simply realize that in Spirit He is now answering my prayer and bestowing upon me His richest gifts. I do not supplicate Him for blessings, but seek to clear my vision and to behold their manifestation.

I know that by prayer, by my aspiring heavenward, I am lifted out of inharmony, disease, and lack. By spiritual communion I identify myself with Spirit within me. I become aware of its presence, its power, its might to overcome every external claim to power. Abiding in the consciousness of these mighty truths, I am in a state of constant prayer, constantly knowing the joys of heaven expressed through God to me. Regardless of the external situation, I can master it through prayer, through realizing Truth.

I will pray with the spirit, and I will pray with the understanding also.—1 Corinthians 14:15

In all situations I resort to prayer
and find my oneness with God.

JANUARY 30, 1938

Have you learned to turn to God in prayer when you need to feel at one with Him and realize that He is present? Do you resort to prayer when appearances of evil present themselves? Is prayer a natural process, something that you do readily, heartily, effectively?

Form the very good habit of resorting to prayer. When some evil thought comes to mind, pray. When sin, evil, fear, hate, disease, or failure seems to prevail, pray in the consciousness that Truth will be established. You will come to know that prayer is not some weird, intangible, impractical religious act, but that it is the most necessary thing in man's experience. You will see that prayer is right thought: thinking of your unity with God.

Find time several times a day to commune with God. Pray in the consciousness that God is with you bestowing good upon you. Pray in the realization that only God can fill your world.

They ought always to pray, and not to faint.—Luke 18:1

I keep my consciousness attuned to God this day
and abide in a spirit of prayer.

OCTOBER 26, 1941

To abide in a spirit of prayer does not necessarily mean that a person has to go apart and sit in the silence for a while, but it means that he is continuously cognizant of his divine heritage of life, light, peace, and supply.

It is not possible to pray too much. Prayer is communion with God and the realization of oneness with Him. We should always abide in this realization; for negation can manifest itself only when we allow ourselves to believe that we are separate from God and His good.

Special periods of prayer are important in every person's life, but it is even more important that we carry over into every moment of our living the consciousness of God's presence that we gain from our periods of prayer and communion. We cannot obtain lasting results by praying for a few moments and then going about our affairs thinking about negative conditions that seem to be present. We should abide in a spirit of prayer by realizing momently that God is at hand.

Pray without ceasing.—1 Thessalonians 5:17

I open my mind and heart to God in prayer, and he gives me light, guidance, and fulfillment.

DECEMBER 28, 1945

Most persons do not pray for enough. That is why they do not experience the great transformations in their life that they hope for.

Most persons base their ideas of what will give them happiness and satisfaction upon what they have experienced in the past and upon what they can observe in the life of other persons. They form their prayers around this experience and around this observation, and many times the answers to their prayers are not as satisfying as they anticipated, because the real need of their soul is beyond what they have yet experienced or yet observed.

Only God can penetrate to the deepest places of the mind and heart and give true and perfect satisfaction. The most effective and most satisfying way of prayer is to set aside your own preconceived ideas when you go to God for help and allow Him to reveal to you the truth about yourself and about your needs. Open your mind and heart to God and He will give you light, guidance, and fulfillment.

My expectation is from him.—Psalm 62:5

From the Readers of Daily Word

I really enjoy Daily Word. *It uplifts me and gives me strength when I need it the most. It is a blessing to me.*

—D.M., CHICAGO

I love it. It has helped me mentally and physically for many, many years. God bless you all.

—J.H., NEW YORK

I couldn't live without my Daily Word.

—G.P., BELTSVILLE, MARYLAND

I take everything to God in prayer, and my life is blessed with health, peace, and plenty.

MARCH 15, 1950

Most of us are familiar with these lines of an old hymn:
"O what peace we often forfeit,
O what needless pain we bear,
All because we do not carry
Everything to God in prayer."

If we are in need of peace of mind, if we feel weak or heavy-laden, if we are discouraged with life we may well follow the advice of this hymn and "take it to the Lord in prayer."

God is a help in every need; God is your help in time of trouble; God hears and answers every prayer.

Let us turn our attention away from external conditions and appearances and joyously seek God's presence within. Let us feel the goodness of God working in and through us and the entire universe. Let us feel the unity of all life. Let us realize that we are one with all that is good. This is true prayer. This is affirmative prayer.

All things, whatsoever ye shall ask in prayer, believing, ye shall receive.—Matthew 21:22

Today I put prayer into practice,
and blessings come to me from everywhere.

JUNE 10, 1957

Some persons feel hesitant about praying. They feel that they have never learned to pray properly and they scarcely know where to begin. Prayer is the most wonderful, and yet the most simple thing in the world. It may be defined as right thought—constructive thought, if you wish—followed by right feelings, right words, and right action.

You can learn to put prayer into practice. Every right thought is a prayer, and prayer is creative. Through prayer your entire life can be changed.

Prayer puts you in tune with God. It makes you a channel through which power and energy flow. It gives you a feeling of being secure and of being wanted and needed by your fellow men. Prayer fills you with an awareness of the love of God.

Keep your heart and mind open and receptive to God's presence by keeping your thoughts and feelings loving and constructive. Place yourself and your every desire in God's care and know that even now His Spirit is blessing you.

Pray without ceasing.—1 Thessalonians 5:17

The spirit of truth guides me in
my prayers for others.

OCTOBER 26, 1961

How do we use affirmative prayers to help others? When we make an affirmation for ourselves we state that which is eternally true of us, and we do likewise when we make an affirmation for another person. Rather than praying about the need of another person—health, supply, guidance, freedom—let us affirm the truth about him and for him.

We do not need to pray to God to bless another person. We need only to lift up our thoughts and know that already God is blessing him! God is within him, the source of all that he can need or desire. Does the one for whom we pray seek healing? God is his life. Does the one for whom we pray seek employment, a home? God is his supply and support. Does the one for whom we pray seek guidance, light, and encouragement? God is the Spirit of truth within him, God is his light, God is the lifting power within him. Whatever our dear ones seek, let us affirm the truth for them. Let us keep faith in the Spirit of God within them.

Lord, teach us to pray.—Luke 11:1

I work with God; God works through me.

JULY 9, 1963

Prayer and action are often separated in our mind. We may feel that the person who says he will pray about a situation or a problem will be doing nothing. Or we may feel that the person who takes action in a situation, makes some motion to solve a problem, is not giving it prayerful thought.

When there is a blending of prayer and action there is the balance that brings about and maintains order. It is possible that after prayer we shall be inspired to wait patiently, relax and let go, doing nothing in an outer way. But it is also possible that after prayer we shall be guided to take a step, proceed in a certain way, enter into some particular activities.

We should always follow the leading that comes to us through prayer. We should realize that life need not always be cast in a certain pattern. We should be flexible. As we co-operate in this way with the power of the universe, we work with God; God works through us.

Go and wash in the Jordan seven times.—2 Kings 5:10

God Bless Them

Theobel Wing Aleeson

God bless them, those I love the best,
Wherever they may be or go—
I know that I have never guessed
The fullness of Thy Love's outflow.

Lord, let me hold no alien thought,
No thought of failure, none of ill;
Let me know truly that their lot
Is glorious if they seek Thy will.

God bless them now in perfect ways.
They are Thy children. In Thy care
Let them walk gladly all their days,
Guided and guarded everywhere!

At all times and in all situations, I am upheld and strengthened by the love of God.

SEPTEMBER 29, 1971

As you read these words, you are one in thought and prayer with a great multitude of other *Daily Word* friends. Do you know that *Daily Word* goes to practically every corner of the world? Wherever there are people there is likely to be someone turning its pages now, seeking reassurance and renewal.

When you affirm the *Daily Word* prayer for the day, you are not only helping and blessing yourself and those near and dear to you; you are also adding your blessing to the many unseen, unknown friends who are praying this same prayer. There is power in united prayer.

As you think about the prayer for today: "At all times and in all situations, I am strengthened and upheld by the love of God," give thanks that this is true. God's love surrounds and enfolds you, strengthens and upholds you. And give thanks too, that this same loving presence is upholding and blessing anyone, anywhere, who needs this strengthening assurance now.

Lo, I am with you always.—Matthew 28:20

I pray for myself and others and
expect perfect answers to my prayers.

JUNE 7, 1979

Sometimes a person asks: "Can I pray for my dear ones even though they are not aware of my prayers, even if they do not believe in the effectiveness of prayer?" Yes, we can pray effectively for others, we can pray for that which is for their highest good, that which is God's perfect answer to their every need.

The prayer that is always a blessing, the prayer that is always effective, is the prayer that recognizes the spiritual self of the one for whom we pray. We pray not to change a person but to bless him by beholding the Christ in him. True prayer brings an inner quickening and a release of divine power.

We pray for light and guidance, for life and health, for freedom and fulfillment, for prosperity and success. We pray, beholding the perfection of God, and change comes about, good comes forth.

The prayer of a righteous man has great
power in its effects.—James 5:16

I pray not to change others but
to change my thought about them.

JANUARY 30, 1982

Have we been anxious and worried about our dear ones? Have we been thinking about their needs, their problems? Have we been seeing them as lacking in wisdom or judgment, as making mistakes, as needing help? Have we been praying for them, asking God to change them, to guide them?

We truly bless others in prayer when we pray not to change them but to change our thought about them, to change our view of them.

True prayer for others sees no need, only God's supply. True prayer sees no faults or failings, only God's perfection. True prayer for others lifts up our vision of them. True prayer for others beholds the Christ in them. True prayer affirms wholeness, strength, wisdom, power, peace, happiness. True prayer for others beholds them as spiritual beings, as children of light. True prayer for others beholds only God, only good, only perfection.

Pray for one another.—James 5:16

Beside the still waters, I am renewed.

JANUARY 31, 1989

The Psalmist wrote, "He leads me beside still waters; he restores my soul." Here, the Psalmist is describing a state of mind that is calm, trusting, and peaceful. In prayer, we are led into such a place. It is through our faith-filled, heartfelt prayers that our minds, our hearts, and our souls are restored.

When we feel weary and tired, our prayers refresh and renew us. When we feel lonely or depressed, our prayers uplift and restore us. When we feel poor and discouraged, our prayers instill in us a feeling of interest and prosperity.

Each day we can take time to pray. It is beside the still waters of prayer that our souls are restored. We arise refreshed and renewed and ready to follow the paths leading to our good, which has already been prepared for us and awaits our acceptance.

The Lord is my shepherd ... He leads me beside still waters;
he restores my soul.—Psalm 23:1, 2-3

I bless the children of the world through my prayers.

APRIL 4, 1991

The children of the world need our love and prayer support. We can help the children whom we know and all the children of the world achieve greater emotional, spiritual, and physical well-being. Today, we give children—the future caretakers of the world—our special prayers and attention.

We continue to hold children in our prayers and to believe in the power of prayer and right thinking. We affirm for each child: *You are God's child, and God is blessing you now.* We envision our affirmations spreading over this planet, blessing children everywhere.

We also include children who are near to us. We can bless by example as well as by words. In our association with children, we demonstrate practical application of divine ideas in daily living. The greatest gifts we can give children are our prayers, love, attention, and encouragement to think, talk, and live according to God's truth.

Let the children come to me.—Luke 18:16

My prayers for others are powerful affirmations of life and well-being.

APRIL 15, 1993

Words are powerful tools for good in blessing ourselves and others.

Words become even more powerful as faith-filled prayers, for prayer is the language of spirituality that empowers us and transcends all limitations of time, space, and conditions.

As we pray for others, we become part of a healing activity. Words of health bathe us in healing light, and we are blessed. Our prayers for others reach out to them, proclaiming health and healing.

Prayer is a spiritual connection that unites us with our loved ones at any time and for any need. Prayer accompanies our loved ones, enfolding them in love and faith. In our prayers for others, we affirm that with God all things are possible for them and all good is available to them.

I hold you in my heart, for you are all partakers with me of grace.—Philippians 1:7

From the Readers of Daily Word

Thank you very much for your thoughts in Daily Word. *It's the first thing I read every morning to start my day.*

—J.D., CARLTON, OREGON

People should read all the daily readings and pray for peace in the world.

—M.K., GRANGER, TEXAS

Reading Daily Word *first thing sets my mind for the day. How much better can it get?*

—P.S., LAKEPORT, CALIFORNIA

My prayers for the world community
bless the family of God.

SEPTEMBER 30, 2002

The people of the world live in many different countries, all separated into territories by lines on a map. In truth, however, there is no separation between the people on Earth.

The world is one great community of the family of God. So there can be no one decision made by any one person that does not in some way affect the lives of others.

As one person, I send a message to the world community through my prayers. The prayers I send transcend all language and cultural barriers.

Just as my prayers for one person can create positive change in that person's life, so do my prayers for my global family to create positive change in the world. The power of the Almighty supports my faith-filled prayers as they move out to bless the world.

Be exalted, O God, above the heavens.
Let your glory be over all the earth.—Psalm 57:5

Prayer by prayer, I enrich my life.

AUGUST 9, 2009

How do I achieve a spiritually centered life? I pray. When I spend time in prayer, I gain a deeper understanding of my true nature. My potential for a richer, fuller life is revealed to me. Through communion with God I become attuned to the divine presence and power within me. I am strengthened and guided to do what is mine to do.

Prayer immerses me in the love of God and opens my heart to meaningful relationships. Prayer brings me new insight so that I more fully express the love within me.

My life is enriched through the power of prayer, which gives me strength, wisdom, and enthusiasm.

Strive for the greater gifts. And I will show you a still more excellent way.—1 Corinthians 12:31

The power of prayer strengthens us all.

AUGUST 1, 2011

Knowing that someone is praying for me encourages me to believe that good is unfolding in my life. Whether I am heading out for a job interview, facing a health issue, or caring for a loved one, it is good to know I have a praying friend holding me up. This turns me away from worry and opens me to the power of affirmative prayer.

Positive prayer energy moves through us as a blessing. It feels good to be spiritually centered, affirming the power and presence of God in our lives. The power of prayer does not change God; prayer inspires and strengthens those who are praying and those who are held in prayer. In the partnership of prayer, all receive benefit from the affirmation of God's indwelling presence.

This is what we pray for, that you may become perfect.
—2 Corinthians 13:9

My life is prayer in action.

MARCH 6, 2016

Unity author James Dillet Freeman wrote, "Prayer is a reaching, and every act of prayer stretches the soul." I can stretch my soul by beginning and ending my day with quiet times of prayer, reflection, and thanksgiving. In between I observe expressions of the Divine—in nature and the kindness of others. I set an intention to be a blessing wherever I am. These are acts of prayer—expressions of my divine nature.

I acknowledge the presence and power of Spirit within. Breathing deeply, I give thanks for divine light that guides me. I recognize the pure life that nourishes and energizes every cell of my body. I open to divine ideas and creative ways to use them. I see myself enfolded in a circle of love and peace. *My life is prayer in action.*

I will pray with the spirit, but I will pray with the mind also.—1 Corinthians 14:15

My open heart comforts the world.

FEBRUARY 26, 2020

Watching the evening news, I may be concerned about events unfolding in my own community or around the world. During challenging times I draw upon spiritual practices that anchor my connection to Spirit within and to the entire human family.

Pausing for prayer and breathing quietly for a few minutes help keep me from descending into the energy of fear or conflict. Instead of getting pulled into negativity or feeling overwhelmed, I view troubling news as calls for prayer and calmly enter into the *peace* of my heart.

I am reminded that God's light shines in my heart for me and for all the world. Affirming the Truth for all beings, I am a soothing presence for others who may wish to take sanctuary in the comfort of my heart.

Let your steadfast love become my comfort according to your promise to your servant.—Psalm 119:76

Messages of
PROSPERITY

Messages of PROSPERITY

The messages of *Daily Word* have helped lift millions out of lack thinking and reminded them of the riches of their divine inheritance. Prosperity begins with divine ideas, and *Daily Word* has affirmed their possibility and promise for 100 years. Prosperity begins in consciousness. It is a state of mind achieved by giving attention to our existing blessings and opening ourselves to receive more. These messages affirm that God is the source of our supply.

Leap Over the Wall

[Uncredited]

OCTOBER 1936

Rarely do we find a person who does not admit in his conversation but he has some barrier before him that delays his progress or hinders his self-expression. The barrier is usually one that is believed to have been erected by other persons willfully and maliciously. To such a person comes this affirmation from the Psalms with a promise of deliverance: "By my God do I leap over a wall" [Psalm 18:29].

To a trained hurdler, barriers are but incidents. They but serve as markers to signalize his progress. To him such barriers exist not for the purpose of impeding him but for the purpose of helping him to show his mastery. Without hurdles he could not be a hurdler. We can see that they are a blessing to him.

"By my God do I leap over a wall." Through a realization of our God-given power to leap we can jump over the barrier that seems to impede our progress. When things loom up in front of us, God gives us power to surmount them. The point in the affirmation does not center in there being a wall but in the fact that it can be leaped over. To the person in the consciousness of obstruction and defeat, a wall blocks his passage. To the individual in the consciousness of surmounting any difficulty away becomes more or less nonexistent.

Many persons go through life seeing a barrier before them. They turn back disheartened only to see another barrier in another direction. They live in a consciousness of barriers and consequently find them in their objective experiences.

Leap over the wall today. The barrier that has seemed to be insurmountable can be surmounted. The wall can be leaped over.

The obstruction in your path can be brushed aside. But one thing is required of you: You must have the consciousness of your God-given power to overcome all difficulty and surmount every barrier.

Do there seem to be impediments to your health? Leap in your consciousness to that higher realization of health which knows no barrier or limitation. Are there seeming obstructions to your success and prosperity? Leap over them. Rise to that higher consciousness that recognizes no obstruction, no defeat, no failure.

The wall that appears before you is but an outpicturing of your belief in the past that things or persons of the world can hinder your progress. When you change this belief, there will no longer be obstructions before you. When you realize that by God's power you can leap over whatever appears before you, you will be able to do so.

Live in the consciousness of inner power, victory, and success. In this consciousness you will be unable to recognize any barriers. In the consciousness of your innate power you will find that you cannot think in terms of defeat. Nothing can impede your progress or thwart your efforts for success when you live in the consciousness that you live and act by the power of God.

Leap over the wall! If in subconsciousness some wall has appeared to check your progress, surmount it. You can do this only by resorting to a higher thought. If you think on the level of barriers, you will find your way barred. If you think higher than barriers, your higher thought will take you over them.

"By my God do I leap over a wall." There is nothing in this statement to indicate that there are some walls too resistant or too high for God. There is no suggestion of an insurmountable wall such as you may have called your own. In fact, the leaping over precedes the wall in the sentence. We almost feel that after we have leaped over something we are to find that it was a wall, that almost after surmounting the impossible we find that it was considered insurmountable.

May it not be true, when we have the consciousness of leaping over walls, that walls no longer exist? When we have the realization of our freedom from obstruction, obstruction will cease to bar our path and progress. We shall find hurdling the barriers of life a very easy matter.

Whatever Good

R.H. Grenville

I sowed a seed of friendliness,
A little thing, so small
It was forgotten instantly.
Today I was amazed to see,
When I returned along that way,
That it had grown so tall.

I whistled for the joy of life
As I went up the trail—
A little private rhapsody

Meant only for my ears and me—
But echo sent a symphony
Back across the vale.

Whatever good you give to life
It hastens to repay—
Not seed for seed, or coin for coin,
But in the lavish way
Of Him who floods the earth with love
Today and every day.

God's will in me is prosperity and abundance.

JULY 26, 1924

"All desire in the heart for any good is really God's desire in us and for us."—*Lessons in Truth* [H. Emilie Cady]

Poverty is no longer considered a virtue. Students of practical Christianity accept God as their unfailing resource, just as they accept God as their life and their strength. We find God through the consciousness of fullness, not through a consciousness of lack.

Your highest desires are but the desires of your own indwelling Spirit, coming into fuller and fuller expression. The will of God in you is always for your highest good and for your fullest supply. Many people retard and limit their prosperity by denying that they should have plenty. You must know the will of God in you and expect your prosperity, before you can bring it into visibility.

Do not think or talk about limited finances. Do not speak of any person or condition as influencing or limiting your supply. Recognize but one will, the will of God in you. Keep attuned to His all-powerful will. Know that it is a power that wills and brings you bountiful prosperity. Keep your consciousness open and receptive to prosperity. The closed mind makes the closed hand.

"I may be prospered by the will of God."
"If ye be willing and obedient, ye shall eat the good of the land."

*Thou art my all-sufficiency in all things,
and my cup of prosperity runneth over.*

OCTOBER 21, 1927

Man should feel that God, his Father, has placed him in position to enjoy every blessing. He should not think that anything is denied him. As the son of God, man is heir to all that the Father has. God's sufficiency is also man's sufficiency.

What a strong realization of prosperity we get when we think of ourselves to be in possession of all that God has! There is nothing more to be desired. We come into possession of blessings which heretofore we had thought of as unattainable.

If one lacks prosperity he should think of the abundance of God, then know that it is his. His supply will come—perhaps from a most unexpected source. Have you a prosperity problem to be solved? Then apply the principles of prosperity. Take your limited thought off your affairs and begin to bless them with thoughts of prosperity.

All sufficiency in all things will be ours when we grasp the full meaning of God's sufficiency for us. We come into unlimited prosperity when we realize this mighty truth.

Ye, having always all sufficiency in everything, may abound unto every good work.—2 Corinthians 9:8

The prospering mind of God fills me with rich ideas, and His prospering presence attends me with prosperity and success.

MARCH 21, 1930

Disabuse your mind of every thought that poverty is your divine inheritance or that as the son of God you are limited in your possessions. God, your Father, bestows upon you the rich ideas of His opulent mind. By these ideas your prosperity is revealed to you.

Even as spiritual ideas are the connecting link between your mind and the mind of God, so the rich ideas of God join you to your prosperity and success. Think of yourself as unified with prosperous ideas and as attended by the spirit of prosperity in all that you do. Give no place in your mind to the belief that lack has any place whatever in your life. Do not think of yourself as unfortunate or as unsuccessful. As the son of God, you are rich—rich in ideas, rich in success.

You are now in your right place in the great universal scheme of life. Your position is assured, and it is one in which you can serve others while they, in turn, compensate you with blessings.

Jehovah made all that he did to prosper in his hand.
—Genesis 39:3

Prosperous ideas implanted in my mind through Christ now direct me to my own prosperity.

APRIL 21, 1936

When you need more prosperity, you naturally turn to some prosperous idea. Prosperity first of all is mental. You cannot attract prosperity and success if your mind is closed to prosperous ideas. The greatest barrier to such ideas is a consciousness of poverty and failure. Many persons are slow in prospering because of the difficulty they experience in getting rid of fixed ideas about lack.

You cannot believe that prosperity is God's will if you still have the slightest belief that poverty is a virtue. You cannot believe in the free circulation of prosperity through your mind and affairs if you believe that any person or situation has power to stop or delay your prosperity. You cannot prosper if you think that God's world has a limited supply of what you need. Live today in the realization that your mind and affairs are charged with prosperity. Accept your prosperity as true.

Beloved, I pray that in all things thou mayest prosper ... even as thy soul prospereth.—3 John 2

My mind is so full of thoughts of prosperity that there is no room for thoughts of lack.

MAY 21, 1943

Today's prayer points out to us an effective method for coping with the unwelcome thoughts that infest our mental household. We can get rid of them by crowding them out, by filling our mind so full of thoughts of prosperity and plenty that there is no room for them to remain.

It is often truly said that thoughts of plenty are the seed from which prosperity grows. The converse is also true, namely that thoughts of lack are the seed from which poverty grows.

If we would be prosperous always, we need to cease thinking about lack or insufficiency of any kind. We need to dwell continually in thought on the truth that God is infinite abundance of every good thing that we can ever need or desire. By continually projecting into our consciousness these prosperous thoughts, we make it impossible for any contrary thoughts to become established there.

Thou sendest forth thy Spirit, they are created;
and thou renewest the face of the ground.—Psalm 104:30

The spirit of prosperity and success has entered into my affairs, and my whole visible supply is abundantly increased.—Unity Prosperity Thought

SEPTEMBER 21, 1948

The spirit of prosperity and success is the divine power of God active in our life and affairs. This Spirit causes our visible supply to increase and become manifest according as we are able to see and understand that its origin and source is in the invisible realm of divine substance.

Our senses tell us we live in a world of materiality, but the divine wisdom within us tells us that underlying this materiality is the living, pulsing energy of God Himself, ceaselessly active, ceaselessly at work in the affairs of men.

As we join in our prosperity thought for the current month, let us affirm it with active faith in its truth. As the conviction grows within us that the Spirit of prosperity and success has entered into our affairs and is now working through the impetus given it by our faith, we shall see our visible supply increase in abundant measure.

Only be strong and very courageous, to observe to do according to all the law ... that thou mayest have good success whithersoever thou goest.—Joshua 1:7

From the Readers of Daily Word

I enjoy reading Daily Word. *It is my quiet time with God.*
—J.M., CUERO, TEXAS

Daily Word *gives me a meditative theme for each day.*
I hold it dear.
—S.A., PINOLE, CALIFORNIA

The Daily Word *has helped me to become calmer, more*
forgiving, and patient. Most of all thank God every day for
what he does for me and for what he did for us all.
—B.M., ALTAMONTE SPRINGS, FLORIDA

All thoughts of lack are eliminated. Prosperity and success are established in mind and affairs, in the name of Jesus Christ.—Unity Prosperity Thought

JANUARY 21, 1951

Prosperity and success come to us not by chance, but because we make ourselves ready for them through sincere and steadfast spiritual preparation.

It is a law of mind action that only one thought pattern at a time can hold precedence in our mind. What we think most strongly becomes manifest for us. It follows logically then that when our thinking is confused, sometimes positive and sometimes negative, the condition of our affairs will depend on whether the positive or the negative thoughts are in the ascendancy.

To insure that prosperity and success become established in our life, we must first prepare the way for them by eliminating all thoughts of lack. We rid ourselves of such thoughts by resolutely affirming our faith in God as instant, constant, and abundant supply. As we continue to follow this practice, prosperity and success are ours.

Prepare ye in the wilderness the way of Jehovah.
—Isaiah 40:3

The spirit of the Lord goes before me this day and prepares the way for my success and prosperity.

NOVEMBER 19, 1956

Charles Fillmore, in his book *Prosperity*, says: "Let us start with the fundamental proposition that there is plenty for you and for me and that the substance is here all the time, supplying us with every needful thing, according to our thought and word …

"When you start to your work, pause a moment and declare: 'The Spirit of the Lord goes before me this day and makes my way successful and prosperous.' Make this your proclamation for the day. Decree it to be so and the Lord will bring it to pass. During the day, if a thought of lack or limitation should for a moment disturb you, banish it at once with the statement; 'Jehovah is my shepherd; I shall not want.'

"Realize most strongly that your prosperity comes from God. It came with you from God. Supply may seem to come through outer channels, but your real success depends on your inner hold on the prosperity realization."

Jehovah is my shepherd; I shall not want.—Psalm 23:1

God, and only God, is the source of my supply.

MARCH 5, 1962

In the past I may have believed that my prosperity was dependent on my work, my business, my inheritance, or my investments. Now I accept the truth that God, and only God, is the source of my supply.

I bless every outer channel of supply but I am not dependent on these channels for my prosperity. I know that God, the Fountainhead of all good, is the true, unfailing source of supply, success, prosperity, and rich, new ideas.

I look to God for my supply. No longer will I believe that any person, place, or outer thing can affect or interfere with my success and prosperity.

In my new understanding there is no room for belief in lack. There is no longer any occasion to doubt that abundance and not lack is my divine heritage from God.

I am established in a constructive, productive state of mind. I am open and receptive to the new, prospering ideas of God and I lay hold of them to increase prosperity in my affairs.

My God shall supply every need of yours.—Philippians 4:19

I am free, praise God, I am free. The prospering power of God pours out on me and fills my every need.
—Silent Unity Prosperity Prayer for July

JULY 15, 1968

Does it seem that there is never quite enough money to meet current needs, to pay bills? We need to free ourselves from fearful thoughts concerning our supply; we need to expand and enlarge our concept of the prospering power of God.

Rather than looking at your finances and seeing lack and limitation, lift up your thought and see plenty—plenty and to spare. Look at your affairs and say to yourself, "God is the source of my good. God is the supplier of my every need, and God is unlimited."

"Prove me now herewith, saith the Lord of hosts, if I will not open you the windows of heaven, and pour you out a blessing, that there shall not be room enough to receive it." "Eye hath not seen, nor ear heard, neither have entered into the heart of man, the things which God hath prepared for them that love him."

I will ... pour you out a blessing.—Malachi 3:10

That Inward Tide

Donna Miesbach

There is a freedom in the wilderness
Of the ocean and the wave
That neither halts nor wavers
Nor seeks the surge to stave

But rather with abandon
Throws itself upon the shore
And thus, in giving all away,
It becomes yet more.

So may that same abandon
Have its way with me.
May all I have and all I give
Flow from a heart so free

That never is there less
But always only more—
The rhythm of that inward tide
On my eternal shore.

The Christ presence abiding in me is now opening new avenues of success and prosperity.

OCTOBER 4, 1974

There may be those who feel that man has gone as far as he can go. They may believe that the human race has drained nature's resources. They may think that there are no new resources to tap, no new ways to supply the growing demand of a growing world. The truth is that God's infinite supply is all about and within man, awaiting his use.

We have the Christ presence in us that is indomitable. The Christ presence abiding in us blesses us with infinite wisdom, unlimited energy and enthusiasm, and the imagination that sees new avenues through which success and prosperity can come forth. The initiative of the Christ presence in us enables us to use what we have—our ideas, our training, the materials at hand—in new and constructive ways.

There is challenge, there is opportunity, there is growth for us, no matter where we are or who we are. Right now, the Christ in us is opening new avenues of success and prosperity to us.

Come; for all is now ready.—Luke 14:17

I know my own shall come to me, for the law of giving and receiving is at work in my life.

MAY 5, 1977

Today's prayer thought contains a truth to ponder. Let us affirm it and then let us take stock of our lives. How can we increase the flow of good into our lives?

What do we have to give? Ideas? Energy? Special training? Talents? Time? Whatever we have to give, as we give it, the way will be opened for our own prosperity to come to us. We need never look at other persons and long for their opportunities, their abilities, their position. We need only consider what is ours to give.

There may be those who feel that their own can come to them without any effort on their part. In some instances this may seem almost to be true. But seeds must be planted to harvest a crop. In order to be prosperous, we must fulfill the divine law of giving and receiving. How and what we give depends on us, but give we must. We make room for our prosperity to come to us by giving whatever it is we have to give.

The harvest is plentiful.—Matthew 9:37

Praise the Lord, whose never-failing abundance prospers me.

NOVEMBER 6, 1985

Charles Fillmore reminds us: "You should expect prosperity when you keep the prosperity law. Therefore be thankful for every blessing that you gain and as deeply grateful for every demonstration as for an unexpected treasure dropped into your lap. This will keep your heart fresh; for true thanksgiving may be likened to rain falling upon ready soil, refreshing it and increasing its productiveness.

"When Jesus had only a small supply He gave thanks for the little He had. This increased that little into such an abundance that a multitude was satisfied with food and much was left over. Blessing has not lost its power since the time Jesus used it. Try it and you will prove its efficacy. The same power of multiplication is in it today. Praise and thanksgiving impart the quickening spiritual power that produces growth and increase in all things."

I follow this advice. I expect and I give praise for prosperity in unlimited measure.

Praise the Lord, for the Lord is good.—Psalm 135:3

> *The resurrecting power of Christ fills me with prospering ideas. I am successful and fulfilled.*

MARCH 29, 1989

Do we connect "if only" statements to our seeming lack of prosperity and success? "If only I had time and money to further my education ... the ways and means to meet the perfect companion ... the opportunity to prove my own value and worth to my family, supervisors, or friends."

When we question our own ability to be prosperous, we are sowing our seeds of prosperity on rocky ground and in thorny places. To be prosperous, successful, and fulfilled, we need to sow our seeds of prosperity in good soil. We do this as we recognize that the resurrecting power of Christ is ours to call upon and use.

The resurrecting power of Christ fills us with prospering ideas. As we use the ideas we receive in times of quiet meditation or busy activity, we are successful and fulfilled.

Other seeds fell on good soil and brought forth grain, some a hundredfold.—Matthew 13:8

The Christ love within inspires me with divine ideas that bless and prosper me.

OCTOBER 19, 1991

In whatever circumstance or area of our lives we reach out with the Christ love, we can be sure of results that include harmony and prosperity.

Before we make an investment of our thoughts, time, finances, or energy, we send the Christ love before us to make our way secure and successful. As we imbue all that we do with the Christ love, we are prospered.

We act on divine ideas not simply to be more prosperous, but for the pure joy of being divine love in expression. Our abundance includes the companionship, finances, well-being, employment, homes, transportation, and security that bring true prosperity into manifestation in our lives. The Christ love within inspires and prospers us.

You, being rooted and grounded in love, may have power to comprehend with all the saints what is the breadth and length and height and depth, and to know the love of Christ which surpasses knowledge.—Ephesians 3:17-19

I am prospered by every thought of God
and by the presence of God.

APRIL 16, 1999

What has brought us our greatest awareness of prosperity probably has nothing to do with financial or material gain.

Learning to read, we were transported to other places and other times while sitting in a classroom or in our own homes. We gained a perspective of the whole world as home.

Holding our children or grandchildren in our arms right after their births, we learned there is no limit to how much we can expand our hearts. We can and do love new life without loving any other life less.

Every time we recognized God's presence within us and within others, we allowed our spiritual understanding to grow and enrich our lives. This is prosperity of the soul.

Yes, yes, we are indeed prospered.

And God is able to provide you with every blessing in abundance, so that by always having enough of everything, you may share abundantly in every good work.—2 Corinthians 9:8

From the Readers of Daily Word

The Daily Word *has been a blessing for me, every time I open it and read it, right on time at the right time, the scripture and the encouraging words that go with it. In 2020 I lost my youngest child. She was 22—died of suicide. Six months later I was diagnosed with breast cancer. But God be the glory—I thank God for his strength holding me up, keeping me up and only God's comforting power.*

—S.D., ELK GROVE, CALIFORNIA

I started reading Daily Word *16 years ago as a gift subscription from my mom, who passed away last year. I always think of her when I read it.*

—K.J., WHITE PLAINS, NEW YORK

> *Expressing my spirituality in a world created by God, I am prosperous.*

DECEMBER 27, 2000

Although I enjoy material things and personal accomplishments, they are not what truly enriches my life.

Expressing my own spirituality does, for then I bring a sacredness to every moment of my life. And I understand how sacred all God's creation is.

So I am not concerned about having more in life. I am dedicated to being more in my own life and in the lives of others. I am honored to be a child of God and to share a spiritual kinship with all people.

My health, my family, and my peace of mind enrich me. Prosperity is all around me! There is so much to appreciate, and giving thanks for even a little leaves me feeling so good! Holding my life and all other life in high regard, I realize how prosperous I am.

The blessing of the Lord makes rich, and he adds no sorrow with it.—Proverbs 10:22

I am open and receptive to the goodness of God and prospered in all I do.

OCTOBER 15, 2006

I ask myself, What shall I be open and receptive to today? If yesterday I allowed my thoughts to be fearful or worrisome, then today I begin by courageously letting go of these worries and fears. Today I lift my thoughts higher. I am open and receptive to the goodness of God. Today my focus and attention are firmly placed on the truth that I am one with my Creator. I am connected to the Source, and in this truth, I embrace the potential that is within me.

Any shadow of doubt has cleared away because I know that prosperity and success are not dependent on outer circumstances. Always having faith that God is the source of inexhaustible good, I openly receive God's supply. I am prospered in all I do.

For the Lord your God is bringing you into a good land, a land with flowing streams, with springs and underground waters welling up in valleys and hills.—Deuteronomy 8:7

My positive thoughts reveal a prosperous world.

SEPTEMBER 20, 2012

I use the power of positive thought to reveal true prosperity in the worlds of form and spirit. As I affirm abundance, I become more aware of the goodness of God in my life.

My prosperous thoughts may prompt the prayer "Thank You, God" as I go about my busy day—or they may fill my mind in meditation as I focus on God's good. My prosperous thoughts may manifest into a treasure map illustrating my goals or in affirmations that reinforce my unlimited potential as a child of God. I create more prosperity for myself, my loved ones, and the world through the power of affirmative prayer.

Whatever is pleasing, whatever is commendable, if there is any excellence and if there is anything worthy of praise, think about these things.—Philippians 4:8

I joyously anticipate new adventures
in prosperous living.

SEPTEMBER 28, 2017

In his book *Spiritual Economics*, Eric Butterworth explained, "The word *prosperity* comes from the Latin root which literally translates: 'according to hope,' or 'to go forward hopefully.' Thus it is not so much a condition in life as it is an attitude toward life."

With this in mind, I focus my thinking on what I want to experience in this adventure called life. If I slip into thoughts of lack, I realign by centering myself again in the peace and assurance of God's love and abundance.

Prosperity is a way of living, of expecting good outcomes, and answered prayers. It is a consciousness of believing in possibilities and going forward in hope. Anticipating new adventures in prosperous living, I give thanks for all I have and for the blessings yet to come.

For surely I know the plans I have for you.—Jeremiah 29:11

I create space for prosperous living.

FEBRUARY 19, 2021

If I want to welcome something in my life, I need to create the conditions necessary for it to manifest. For instance, saying I want a loving relationship is not enough. I must be open and receptive to love.

Craving comfort and security while dwelling on what I lack is akin to building a wall between me and all I desire. Removing the obstacles I have placed in the way of togetherness automatically brings me closer to others, and relationships naturally grow.

Spending time in gratitude for what I already have gives me a prosperous mindset, and more to appreciate easily comes my way.

I cultivate abundance by focusing my feelings and thoughts on the flow of limitless substance. I am prosperous beyond measure.

The plans of the diligent lead surely to abundance.
—Proverbs 21:5

Messages of GUIDANCE

Messages of
GUIDANCE

Guidance is one of the most frequently requested prayer topics at the Unity Prayer Ministry and a favorite of *Daily Word* readers too. Part of the human condition is asking, "What's next?" and looking for light on the path. Wherever the crossroads and whatever the decisions that are being faced, divine wisdom within is available to illuminate our next steps.

How to Have a Conversation with God

By Janet Conner

MARCH/APRIL 2010

During my first careers as teacher, recruiter, and consultant, if someone had said, "You're going to write a spiritual book," I'd have burst out laughing. Little did I know that my invitation from Spirit was coming. It came in the form of a brutal divorce.

One morning, out of sheer desperation, I scribbled "Dear God," across the top of a journal page.

As I made the comma, a torrent of angry, frightened words piled up inside my pen. My story poured itself onto page after page. Venting felt good, so the next day, I wrote another diatribe to "Dear God." After several days of barking at God, I wrote a question—a question I didn't even know was inside me: "How did this happen? What have I been unwilling to see?" With these questions my monologue ended and a divine dialogue began.

For three years, I wrote to Dear God every day. I noticed something. If I asked for guidance, guidance came. If I asked for insight, insight came. When I asked for comfort, I was comforted. When I asked for protection, my son and I were safe. When I needed financial help, it came. I talked with Dear God about everything in my life—big and small.

Does that sound miraculous? It is. It's miraculous how soul writing activates the Voice of Spirit. But it's a miracle you can do. Here's how.

Soul Writing

Set your intention to connect with Spirit. Write by hand. (The computer keeps you in conscious mind and you want to get out of your stress-filled conscious mind.) Write directly to

Spirit using your favorite name. Speak from the heart. Write fast.

Writing fast gets you out of the way so Spirit can break through.

Ask questions. Open-ended questions are the magic that activates the Voice. As your conversation for the day ends, say thank you. Be grateful for the experience.

New soul writers always ask me: Am I talking to God or to myself? Eyebrows sometimes scrunch when they hear my answer: The Voice is that which is inside you that is greater than you. But, they press, is that Spirit?

Yes, I smile, it's Spirit. It is the limitless source of wisdom, creativity, guidance, and grace. But, please understand, it is also you. The Voice is Spirit in you.

That answer provokes my favorite question: How will I recognize the Voice? I love this question because it gives me the opportunity to watch people's faces as they hear the sweet sound of the Voice, perhaps for the first time.

I recognize the Voice on my own pages when a new thought, idea, or question I haven't considered tumbles out or when the pen gleefully flies over the paper. Other soul writers see shifts in their handwriting, feel tingles in their hands or a sensation of warmth in their heart. But we all agree on one thing: The Voice is unmistakable because it speaks its own language—the language of unconditional love.

Let me give you one example. Jody, a 36-year-old woman in Florida, was with her mother every day of a nine-year struggle with cancer. Jody said they were more than mother and daughter; they were best friends and soul mates. When her mother died, Jody felt lost. She came to my workshop hoping to find some peace.

In her very first 10-minute writing experience, the Voice burst through her confusion and tears to say in distinctive capital letters, "I AM UNBREAKABLY YOURS." After everyone left, Jody showed me the page. In tears, she said, "This is the Voice, isn't it?" "Oh yes," I sighed, "this is the unmistakable sound of the Voice of Love."

Would you like to hear that sweet Voice of Love?

Pick up a pen and say, "I'm here." The Voice will find you. "Hello beloved," it will say. Welcome to the conversation that never ends—it just goes deeper and deeper to your whole, authentic, holy self. "I'm so glad you're here. Let's talk."

Janet Conner is the author of several books including *Writing Down Your Soul* about the power and practice of deep soul writing.

Affirmation at Dawn

Elizabeth D. Schumann

The love of God flings wide the gates of day
And bids me rise to walk His perfect way.
The life of God now fills my soul with power
And flows in beauty through each radiant hour.
His wisdom plans full answer to my need;
Guides and directs each thought and word and deed.
His substance is the source of boundless good.
His grace inspires my heart to brotherhood.

Thus shall I find contentment and release
Walking with God in plenitude and peace.
No doubt or fear shall hold my eager feet
From climbing to heights of faith. I greet
This new day in the glow of Spirit's light,
And go forth unafraid to meet the night;
For I have talked with God this glorious dawn—
His love, His strength, His purpose lead me on!

I am free from indecision. The wisdom of God directs me into that which is for my highest good.

JANUARY 14, 1926

Indecision is at the basis of much confusion and disorder. The ability to arrive at a right decision comes through single-mindedness, that consciousness in which one realizes that there is but one path and, consequently, one decision. When one is centered in Truth he knows but one way—that which will bring him the highest good. Instead of the darkness of indecision, the light of understanding and of wisdom illumines his path.

Indecision shows that one is working entirely with outer conditions. In doing this, one has presented to him various ways and methods. Contrary to this way of working is that of handling conditions and situations from the standpoint of Truth.

In order to perceive things from the higher consciousness, one must first get so still that he ceases to reason about many ways and many decisions; then in the inner quietness he perceives the truth about the situation. He sees that there is but one thing to do. The light of truth so illumines the one path that he sees but one direction in which to move.

"Another form of thought related to judgment is the vacillating mind which never seems to know definitely what is the proper thing to do."—*Christian Healing* [Charles Fillmore]

Purify your hearts, ye doubleminded.—James 4:8

The light of God has scattered the darkness of ignorance and indecision. God in the midst of me radiates light upon my path.

JANUARY 13, 1928

God at the center of my being is my light and understanding. Darkness, ignorance, and indecision are now put to flight. There are no shadows before me, neither are there obstacles upon my path.

God in the midst of me is my light and understanding. I know that I can lean upon God when I need help. I can rely upon His wisdom when I am undecided or uncertain as to which step I should take.

Trusting in God and in His light, I am free from all fear of darkness—the darkness of an unenlightened consciousness. I am secure in the light and the wisdom that put darkness and shadows to flight.

Trusting in the light of God, I have all the intelligence that I need. The light of spiritual consciousness is shed upon my way, and my feet are guided in the right direction. The Spirit of God ever attends me and directs me into my highest good.

I understand God's will and I am willing to be led into the way which He has chosen for me. There is but one path before me, the way which He has chosen for me, the path which will bring me to success.

Trust in Jehovah with all thy heart, and lean not upon thine own understanding.—Proverbs 3:5

My spiritual consciousness now opens for me the way of Spirit, the way of peace, love, health, success, and plenty.

AUGUST 9, 1936

Have you found your way in life? Do you always seem to choose the right path? Have you learned to turn to Spirit for guidance and direction? Have you discovered that you need not go the way of sacrifice and denial and failure? The way of Spirit opens before you when you discover it in spiritual consciousness. You discover that God's way for you is the way of wisdom, peace, light, good, joy, and plenty.

In Truth there is but one way, the way of Spirit. We find this way when we find Spirit. We discover that the presence of Spirit attends us in all our ways when our thought is centered upon Spirit alone. We find that we are led into paths of peace and success when we let ourselves be led by our indwelling Spirit.

Your way will be one of joy and plenty when you turn to Spirit. You will no longer go the adverse way. You cannot know indecision when you let Spirit direct you in what you do.

The God of Jacob ... will teach us of his ways, and we will walk in his paths.—Isaiah 2:3

The Spirit of wisdom now directs me to take the path that leads me to the blessing I seek.

FEBRUARY 6, 1937

Think of the wisdom of God as having specific bearing upon whatever you seek in life. Know that you are led into your highest good through being guided into the path that the Spirit of wisdom has selected for you. Realize that this path leads you into peace, joy, and success.

Your way is blessed by God when you discover His way for you. You realize that there is no other way in Truth but the way of God. You see that other paths are but detours leading circuitously away from the path of Truth. The path of Spirit is that which followed according to spiritual direction will lead you to your highest good.

Let your indwelling Spirit guide you into the path you should take at this time. Rely upon this guidance. Go the way of Spirit if you expect spiritual blessings. Choose the path of Spirit in place of paths that lead to bondage and limitation. The way of Spirit can bring you naught but that which will inspire, bless, and heal. Only good can come to you when you go the way of Spirit.

Make straight paths for your feet.—Hebrews 12:13

God has need of me, and he guides me to the places and persons I can best serve.

NOVEMBER 1, 1945

With men returning from the war, with the shift from warmaking to peacemaking, there will be adjustments to be made, there will be many persons in need of guidance regarding their right placement as to work and home.

If you are in need of such guidance or if you would help someone in need of such guidance, let your help and your prayer be based on the idea that there is a right place for every one of God's children, a place where he can be happy and successful, where he can give expression to his particular abilities. Every one of us is needed; we are more important than we realize. And when we open our mind to the idea that there is a right place for us, we open the way for our guidance into this place.

The development of our special capabilities, whatever they may be, our interest in life and in the world about us, helps us create a place for ourselves, helps us to be happy wherever we find ourselves.

Guide our feet into the way of peace.—Luke 1:79

Today I seek God's guidance in all things.

NOVEMBER 2, 1948

Today the people of America are electing a president. We believe that everyone in every nation is interested in this election, and we ask for the prayers of all our friends that the people of America may make a wise choice.

Let us who vote today pray for guidance and know that our vote carries a blessing. God in His divine wisdom helps us to make right decisions and to judge righteous judgment.

Because of the great need for order, peace, and harmony among men and nations we pray earnestly and sincerely each day—as do countless numbers of people the world over—that order may be established in our country and in every country. We pray that the leaders of all nations may be unified in thought, purpose, and understanding for the good of all humanity.

God is omnipresent and omnipotent, and there is nothing to fear about the future of the world. As we seek God's guidance today we know that there is nothing to fear as regards the outcome of the election.

[President Harry S. Truman was elected over Thomas Dewey.]

The law is light.—Proverbs 6:23

From the Readers of Daily Word

Daily Word *is a blessing to my life. In all the years I am reading, I also send the book to my friends and it has changed their life.*

*—*A.D., BROOKLYN, NEW YORK

On a day by day, the scriptures meet the events as they are happening. It gives hope to sometimes events that appear inevitable. It gives hope when there appears no hope. Thank God for Daily Word *and all the hope its scriptures present.*

*—*O.E., MISSOURI CITY, TEXAS

Daily Word *each day gives us direction and hope in the troubled world we have now.*

*—*G.P., ROCKFORD, ILLINOIS

I look to the spirit of God within me for guidance in finding my own work, my own channel of supply.

JULY 5, 1950

I know that there is a place for me to work where I can be of service and be adequately compensated for my services. I know that there is always a way for me to use my abilities and to express myself in life so as to earn the supply I need.

I do not allow myself to be discouraged or depressed by conditions that appear to be barriers to my good. I keep my faith centered in the source of my good, God, and I draw inspiration, self-knowledge, and guidance from this source. I give the energy of my mind to choosing the persons to contact and the efforts to make in order to claim my own work, my own channel of supply.

Whenever misgivings cloud my faith I turn to the clarifying spirit within me. Whenever conditions deny me self-expression and supply, I turn to the guiding spirit within me. I know that it is from this source that I receive the knowledge and guidance I need to find satisfying self-expression and adequate supply.

Then thou shall make thy way prosperous.—Joshua 1:8

Here I am, Lord. Illumine me, guide me,
show me thy will and thy way.

FEBRUARY 17, 1956

All of us long for a sure and certain guide when we have decisions to make, when we do not seem to know which way to turn. If we only but realized it, we have with us, always, a most dependable, a most unfailing guide. We have God's own Spirit within us. We need not look to other persons for guidance, we have only to look to the one presence and one power that abides with us.

Jesus said, "Neither shall they say, Lo, here! or, There! for lo, the kingdom of God is within you." In time of doubt, in time of decision, let us remember that God is with us, that His intelligence acts through us, that the way is made clear and bright before us as we listen to and heed His voice.

If we need guidance now, let us still our bodies, still our minds, still our emotions, and turn to God in silent prayer, saying "Here I am, Lord. Illumine me, guide me, show me Thy will and Thy way." We shall find, as we turn first to God for help, that help from persons and outer sources will come to us as it is needed.

The kingdom of God is within you.—Luke 17:21

God's wisdom is now at work in you,
leading you to your highest good.

SEPTEMBER 14, 1962

How can we help someone who has an important decision to make? Should we persuade him to do what seems best to us, or can we help him more by encouraging him to consider all aspects of the situation in the light of God's wisdom within him?

When a friend or a loved one seems to be choosing the wrong course, it is not easy to keep from suggesting what we feel is a better course. But we cannot know what is really best for another person. And in trying to make decisions for him, we deprive him of the opportunity to grow.

We help another person most by freeing him to the all-knowing, all-seeing guidance of His loving Father-God. We help him most by affirming that his own inner wisdom is now at work, leading him to make right decisions. We help him most by helping him learn to call on that divine guidance that is always available to him, now and in any time of need.

Jehovah will guide thee continually, and satisfy thy soul in dry places, and make strong thy bones.—Isaiah 58:11

I stand fast in the faith that there is justice for all.

SEPTEMBER 29, 1969

"Is it wrong to take this to court?" "Should I, as a Truth student, prosecute?" The answer to such questions is found in the fundamental approach of Unity, which is that in all things we are to pray for guidance. As we pray to be shown the way, the particular steps we should take will be revealed.

Justice should prevail in the life and affairs of men. When we find ourselves in the midst of a situation that seems unjust, we have work to do, prayer work. We need to cleanse our mind and heart of any sense of injustice, to affirm that God's law of justice is at work.

With divine guidance we will know what we should do. We will know how to handle each situation wisely, lovingly, kindly, firmly. It is a matter of seeking God's guidance. With our mind open to light and understanding, we will do the right thing, take the proper action, action based on a faith that produces just conditions for all concerned.

Cleanse the inside of the cup and of the plate, that the outside also may be clean.—Matthew 23:26

In This New Day

Dorothy Pierson

Break the fast of night!
Sound a trumpet of joy!
Day has dawned,
The light has come,
The light-line in the east
Has begun the new experience.

Nothing can destroy
The inner peace of this new day.
Begin it quietly, if you will;
Softly let its light distill
Upon you.
Let it unfold
Like the rose outside the window.

Let the light of God,
In its perfect way,
Guide and direct you
In this new day.

*I affirm, "Let there be light," and
I expect to be shown what to do.*

NOVEMBER 30, 1970

My heart sings a song of praise today.

When I have a need for guidance, when it is difficult to know how to proceed in some situation, I turn the whole matter over to God. I let go my anxiety or worry. I let go my feeling of personal responsibility for the right outcome. I say: "Here I am Lord, seeking to know the right way, asking for light and guidance. Let Your light shine into this situation. Make straight the path and make clear the way. I am trusting absolutely in Your light and wisdom. All is well with me and with every situation in my life, for You are here. Your power is at work, Your good is being brought forth."

Having turned every need for guidance or direction over to the loving Spirit of God within me, I am free and at peace. I do the things at hand for me to do. I carry on my regular activities with a calm and trusting spirit. I know that I am being guided step by step. I trust the innate wisdom within me. I expect to be shown what to do.

Then shall your light rise in the darkness.—Isaiah 58:10

Eagerly I seek divine inspiration.
Attentively I listen for spiritual guidance.

MARCH 14, 1976

A preschool child had been chosen to be the "leader" for the day. But being quite a talker, the little fellow talked when he should have been listening. As a result, he was sent to the "thinking room." His grandmother remarked: "If he gets sent to the thinking room often enough, he will end up being a mastermind."

Sometimes all of us talk when we should be listening or act when we should be thinking.

Do we not all have a need (sometimes a greatly neglected need) to repair to our own inner sanctuary, our thinking room, where we become receptive to divine inspiration and guidance?

We can learn to mastermind our own life through prayer, through listening for spiritual guidance, and through lovingly and obediently carrying out the inspiration that comes to us.

I will instruct you and teach you the way you should go;
I will counsel you with my eye upon you.—Psalm 32:8

In this new year I pray, "Here I am, Lord. Use me."

JANUARY 10, 1983

In the Scriptures young Samuel opened himself to the guidance of Spirit by saying: "Speak, Lord, for thy servant hears." He followed the guidance the inner voice brought and became a great judge. In my quiet time I, too, listen for divine guidance from Spirit. I am open and receptive to the inner voice and sincerely seek to be a productive channel of expression. I bring the gift of myself, offered in loving service. My prayer is, "Here I am, Lord. Use me."

I trust in God's plan of good for my life, for I know that it fulfills the divine blueprint of my life. I am thankful for the impact of God-action upon all that is part of my world, insuring that greater good than I have dreamed of will be forthcoming.

God is my life, my supply, my constant joy. I keep my thoughts stayed on truth and allow my life to be used as a channel through which God's love freely flows.

And he said, "Here I am."—1 Samuel 3:6

I am in tune with God, and right answers come to me.

FEBRUARY 8, 1985

There are times when I strive for guidance and direction so fervently that I actually shut it out. Instead of going over and over the problem, it is well to first get in tune with God. My oneness with God enables me to feel my oneness with the order of the universe and all of life. I am then able to pray joyously and effectively.

When I am in tune with God, I am at peace. I am not easily distracted or upset by trivial happenings. I trust God to bring right answers when they are needed and in the way they are needed.

I set the tone for the day when I affirm that I am in tune with God. Any time during the day that I need steadiness of thought and spirit, I return to my affirmation. When I am in tune with God right answers come as easily and as naturally as breathing.

And the Lord will guide you continually, and satisfy your desire with good things.—Isaiah 58:11

I will speak positive words that are inspired by inner guidance.

APRIL 9, 1990

Words are powerful tools. They encourage and heal. They convey understanding and establish unity between people. When they are inspired by inner guidance, our words can be just the blessings that others need to receive. Words that are directed by Spirit unlock doors within our own minds and hearts so that the light of God may shine forth.

As we choose our words today, we do so knowing that they will impart comfort and bring understanding to light. As we allow God's spirit within to guide our words, divine ideas will manifest through them. We know that God works through our words to bring needed blessings to a friend, a coworker, or a stranger.

Our positive instructions, conversations, letters, and other communications are prompted by inner guidance. Our words carry with them the blessing of God's wisdom and love.

For the Holy Spirit will teach you in that very hour what you ought to say.—Luke 12:12

Divine love motivates me to take right action.
I am directed to my highest good.

FEBRUARY 1, 1992

Divine love directs us to the employment, companionships, and endeavors that are especially fitted to our needs. We recognize the guidance of divine love, for it directs us in such a smooth and unerring manner that we pay attention to the most gentle inner promptings.

Many times during this day, we will make decisions. Some seem infinitely more important than others, yet divine love directs us through each and every question that arises. In the silence of prayer, we receive guidance, and we follow the guidance that we receive.

The love of God is directing us to our highest good, and we listen closely. It may be a detailed plan or a flash of inspiration. No matter how it comes, we know that divine love motivates us to take right action as we make our choices today.

Thou dost guide me with thy counsel.—Psalm 73:24

From the Readers of Daily Word

I read each daily message as part of my morning prayers. I keep the back page with positive affirmations for my references.
—S.Q., SOUTH LAKE TAHOE, CALIFORNIA

I always look forward to my subscription arriving; they always have timely words.
—D.S., FERGUS FALLS, MINNESOTA

I feel like the thought of the day is just for me. It helps me be thankful for all of my blessings. It reminds me that God is with me always and He takes me right where He wants me to go.
—S.S., FORT WAYNE, INDIANA

I welcome opportunities to practice trusting my God-given intuition.

SEPTEMBER 29, 2001

On a sunny morning, I may follow an inner prompting to bring along my umbrella. Later, when I am sheltered from an unpredicted shower, I am glad I followed my intuition!

Because I recognize that inner voice as God speaking to me, I do what my intuition calls me to do—even when, at first, that guidance may not seem to make sense. I trust that the rightness of this divine guidance will reveal itself to me in due time.

I gain confidence as I use my intuition in small matters, such as taking a different route to work. I may discover that this decision to vary my route kept me from being delayed in traffic. When a more momentous decision is before me, I act confidently on the opportunity, knowing that God is there to guide me.

Lead me in your truth, and teach me.—Psalm 25:5

I am guided by God to the fulfillment of my dreams.

SEPTEMBER 18, 2007

Looking at the heavens, in the dark of night, I may seek the North Star to locate other diamondlike stars in a black velvet sky. Driving in a new neighborhood, I may refer to the technology of a GPS finder to get my bearings. Assembling a child's toy, I follow directions provided in a language I understand.

Whatever my experiences may be as I seek answers, I am always aware of and drawn to the most powerful source of guidance there is: the presence of God.

God's guidance is always flowing to me and through my experiences in life. I welcome the wisdom of my Creator in making choices and in realizing what emerges from them.

In making plans, taking actions, and fulfilling my dreams, I confidently trust in the wisdom of God.

When they saw that the star had stopped,
they were overwhelmed with joy.—Matthew 2:10

One with the mind of God, I am clearly guided.

JULY 9, 2012

If in the past I have sought God's guidance only for major life decisions or in times of crisis, I remind myself that no need or situation is too small for divine direction.

During my routine activities, I periodically pause to quiet my thoughts and open myself to divine ideas, wisdom, and guidance. I turn my attention inward and silently affirm: *God is with me always and in all things.* Affirming this short statement of Truth opens me to receive whatever I need. An inner knowing may come in this very moment or unfold over time.

Whether my day is crowded with work and appointments or spent in quiet solitude, I am receptive to divine guidance. I live today with the confidence and joy of knowing the mind of God is active within me.

Trust in the Lord with all your heart.—Proverbs 3:5

I open my mind to divine inspiration.

MARCH 20, 2018

Myrtle Fillmore wrote, "You would not think of closing your eyes and walking around saying that you can't see and don't know where you are going. So why close your eye of omniscience by saying, 'I do not know what to do?' Repeatedly affirm that you do know!" With this sage advice, Myrtle reminds us it is never about asking some outside force for guidance; it is remembering and affirming our ever-present connection within divine mind.

Connecting within my sacred heart space, I allow a feeling of curiosity to guide me along as I find confidence for my next steps. I relax into the Silence where I have constant access to divine guidance. With steadfast faith, I follow where I am guided.

Let your good spirit lead me on a level path.—Psalm 143:10

I trust my guidance and feel peaceful and comforted.

OCTOBER 7, 2021

The best way I can distinguish inner guidance from the activity of a busy mind is to notice my feelings. When faced with a decision, do I feel anxious and fearful? Calm and peaceful? Do I feel uneasy and apprehensive or do I feel excited and eager? I trust that feelings are signals showing me my true path, inspired by inner guidance.

I may consider the opinions of others, facts and other data, and my personal history when making choices. Each has its place in the decision-making process, but none is more important than inner guidance.

I remember times when I felt guided to make an unlikely choice, how I trusted my inner voice to lead me in new directions. Today I renew my trust and again follow my guidance.

You are indeed my rock and my fortress;
for your name's sake lead me and guide me.—Psalm 31:3

Messages to LET GO AND LET GOD

Messages to LET GO AND LET GOD

One of the great teachings of Unity is the practice of release. We can only make room for more good by releasing what no longer serves us. Like cleaning out a closet, we sift through a lifetime of behaviors, habits, and thought patterns, discerning what to keep and what to let go. Freed from the past and our limited expectations, we are open to opportunity and unexpected outcomes that are better than we could have imagined.

Let God Handle All

By Mary L. Kupferle

APRIL 1991

Does something in your life seem out of control, dear friend? If so, it is time to let God handle it. Whether it is an emotional upset, a mental block, a physical challenge, or a relationship problem, the solution for each is the same: Let go! Let God handle all!

Perhaps you feel burdened with responsibility because you are the one who usually takes charge in your home, business, or family affairs. Begin now to release your burden by accepting that the most effective way to be in charge is to let God handle it. Regardless of the situation, your own personal involvement, or any need for help or healing, God will reveal the answers and show you the way.

Begin the process of healing now by taking this idea deep into your heart: *I am willing to let go and let God handle all.* Relax your entire being as much as you are able and affirm quietly: I *acknowledge that there is a presence and power beyond my understanding, ready to work through me as I let go. I am willing to let go every struggle to attain a goal on my own. I know that, although of myself I can do nothing, with God all things are possible. I am willing to let go and let God handle all.*

Yes, dear friend, God's infinite wisdom is available to you right now. God's guidance and direction are at hand this very moment to lift you out of every stressful situation, out of the most impossible-to-solve dilemma. Your healing, peace, and strength are right where you are. There is no old habit of anxiety, no old bondage to feelings of loss or doubt that can stand against God's love for you.

> # Remind yourself quietly, again and again: *I am willing to let go and let God handle all.*

As you begin to let go of trying to control challenges, remember that this does not mean that you are shirking your part in the corrective process. Rather, it means that you are courageously facing challenges that have seemed overwhelming. You are facing them with a new awareness of your partnership with God and God's presence and power within you. It means that you are beginning to accept that you *can* handle whatever confronts you because of the solid foundation of God's spirit within you.

Remind yourself quietly, again and again: *I am willing to let go and let God handle all.* If there is some action to take, some word to speak, some truth to know, it will be revealed and accomplished through the guidance of God. You will find that you are not alone, that God's wisdom is supplementing your growth and understanding, that God's love is continually at work for your highest good.

If doubts persist—if you think that you do not know how to do something, that you do not know the answers, that you do not feel that you can forgive, that you do not understand how God can love or help you—respond to each negative thought or feeling with the same quiet affirmation: *I am willing to let go and let God help me. God is the worker, and I am the channel. I know that God can handle everything ...*

Letting go and letting God handle things sometimes means finding new ways of helping yourself to the peace you earnestly desire or the greater health and wholeness you seek. It is important to be willing and obedient to the guidance that comes to you—even as simple nudges or quiet urgings ...

Let go and let God handle any such indication of change. Let God reveal new methods for accepting your good. Letting go and letting God will help you remain flexible and remember that you are ever progressing within the safe yet unlimited scope of God's healing presence and power. Doing so will allow you to think new thoughts without feeling threatened by conditions or circumstances. God is leading you into a wonderful awareness of the peace, light, and love everywhere present that is ready to be called upon, recognized, and accepted ...

I have found, personally, that during times when I have known and understood the least—about how some solution is possible, how a healing can be realized, how peace can be experienced in spite of life's demands, how faith can be recharged when at its lowest ebb, how the right words will come when none spoken before have helped—through persistently letting go and letting God handle it all, the answers and light have become apparent.

Yes, dear friend, you can let go in confidence—let go of every preconceived idea and method in order to more fully let God handle all in wisdom and love for you now. Take time to relax physically, mentally, and emotionally. Repeat the words: *I am willing to let go and let God handle all.* Let these words become a firm basis for everything you need to do to find new peace, strength, healing, faith, courage, and happiness in life.

God Is Love

James Dillet Freeman

If God is love, may I not be?
Did that love not mother me
When God gave my spirit birth
And made me out of clayey earth?

If God is mind, how was I wrought?
Did God think a human thought
And express it in this warm
Flesh that is my human form?

Mother Love and Father Mind,
You and I are intertwined;
When I look for what is true
Of me, I find that it is You.

Established in the high consciousness of Truth,
I have power to rise above every adverse situation.

JANUARY 30, 1927

I am now free from every adverse belief which would bind me to limited conditions. I refuse to be tempted to lose the high vision of my supreme mastery. I stand stabilized in the truth of my victory over all circumstances.

God in the midst of me shows me the way out of every difficulty. The way of God is my way of victory. God's methods are my methods.

Standing on the high pinnacle of Truth, I view all things in their proper relationship. There is nothing too gigantic for God to overcome. Nothing that I need to do is too difficult for me to perform. I can do all things through Christ.

The truth of God is now made clear to me and reveals just what I should do in every situation. The Truth is mighty to release me from every enslaving thought.

The truth of God gives me power over all things of my world. Truth points the way for me, and I walk in the freedom of Spirit.

God is faithful, who will not suffer you to be tempted
above that ye are able; but will with the temptation
make also the way of escape.—1 Corinthians 10:13

The Spirit of the Lord is upon me and I am healed.

MAY 20, 1927

When spiritual consciousness descends into man's body, he is healed. When the high, dynamic, spiritual thoughts that he has understood take root in his physical organism, healing results.

Sometimes when one sits in silent meditation there seems to be a downpour of spiritual glory upon him. At one time he may have believed that this baptism of the Holy Spirit came from some source external and above him. If he has grasped spiritual truth he knows that this baptism is from his own spiritual consciousness and descends from his own mind.

This spiritual baptism tends to clear the mind of all perverted beliefs, all beliefs opposite to spiritual truth. When the thoughts which have caused a tense mentality give way, tension ceases in the body; stagnation and congestion cease; new life flows unimpeded to the various parts of the body.

Man is healed when he lets go of offending beliefs and lets God do his spiritual and healing work.

The Spirit of the Lord is upon me ... He hath sent me to proclaim release to the captives and recovering of sight to the blind, to set at liberty them that are bruised.—Luke 4:18

Established in the justice of God, I am justly dealt with, and I deal justly with all men.

FEBRUARY 15, 1931

I surrender every belief in injustice in order the more fully to understand, possess, and enjoy the justice of God. I give up every thought that I am unjustly dealt with or that any one is now in position to render judgment against me.

Established in the consciousness of divine justice, I deal justly with all whom I contact. I no longer have any desire to be unjust. I wipe from mind every thought that I can succeed through injustice. I cease to believe that I have any right to be unjust with others. I abide in the consciousness of perfect justice.

I know that even now God is at work in me and in all my affairs, bringing justice to pass. I realize that God in the midst of me is mighty to judge wisely, lovingly, justly, and well. I am willing to stand aside and let God do His perfect work. I have no desire to usurp the place of God or to set myself up as a divine judge. Infinite justice now prevails in me and in all my affairs. The justice of God is now manifest in all that I do. His justice prevails in all my dealings, for all my affairs are in His keeping.

What doth Jehovah require of thee, but to do justly.
—Micah 6:8

The life of God permeates my body, His tranquil spirit invests my mind, and I relax and let go.

OCTOBER 1, 1938

When we have responsibilities, it is well to begin our day in a spirit of relaxation. Nothing will so help us to relax as the realization that God is with us and will be guiding us in all that we do and say, arranging our affairs in perfect order. Relax and know that the life of God is infusing you with the energy necessary to the tasks that lie ahead of you. Teach every part, every muscle, of your body to relax and let go. Let every tissue, every nerve, every cell of your body relax and be receptive to the inflowing life of God. In silent communion with God there is relaxation for your mind as well as your body. Let all thought of responsibilities drop away. Open your mind to the inflow of His Spirit. Then nothing will have power to make you tense, for you will be relaxed in the assurance that God is taking care of your affairs.

Rest, and be still.—Jeremiah 47:6

> *I surrender old thoughts, old ways, and old conditions to God. I will to do his perfect will.*

JUNE 26, 1942

Since I have attuned myself to the Father's will, I am not tempted to place my whole happiness and well-being in outer things and outer conditions. I know the importance of following the Christ within.

Through my freedom of will I can reject all that is unlike His perfection. I can accept His light, His life, His plenty, and His divine instruction.

Whereas before I might have hesitated to pray, "Thy will be done," I now realize that I can ask nothing finer, truer, higher than that His will be done in and through and for me. His will is always for my happiness, my health, my prosperity, my good. So I will to do His perfect will.

I praise and give thanks for the "gift of Jehovah," free will. Through wise use of this faculty I now enter the kingdom prepared for me, and I abide in happiness.

Old thoughts and old conditions are now replaced by God's will of abundant good.

The will of the Lord be done.—Acts 21:14

The very spirit of God possesses my mind and heart, and I am filled with his peace and power.

AUGUST 29, 1946

When you let go of personal concern and striving and let the Spirit of God possess your mind and heart, your whole being is flooded with the consciousness of peace and power. Problems, however large or small, drop away from you as you let His Spirit work in and through you.

Whenever you feel you need more wisdom, love, courage, or strength, become quiet and know that He is in possession of every thought. If doubt or fear try to take possession, hold to the realization that God is the only presence and power in your life. You can never be unsure of your way when God's intelligence possesses your mind. You can never be unloving or inharmonious in your relations with others when God's love possesses your heart. You can never be weak or afraid when the consciousness of God's power and might fills every part of your being. As you let go and let God you will be able to meet every experience with poise and confidence.

Casting all your anxiety upon him.—1 Peter 5:7

From the Readers of Daily Word

It's a light that shines bright for me carrying God's words to help me through the day and night. It's given me courage throughout all the body healing and healings of my brain.

— G.S., MARINA, CALIFORNIA

Daily Word *is my connection and guidance to that inner peace we all need to access daily! I never miss a day of inspiration from its authors. Thank you.*

— R.H., MIMS, FLORIDA

It's helped me have better days—enjoy more and have a stronger faith with less worry! It can change your negative outlook to positive!

— K.S., RICHFIELD, MINNESOTA

I learn to let go and let God.

JUNE 14, 1951

How much more smoothly my life goes when I let go and let God help. I do not have to solve my problems by myself; I need not carry my burdens or those of my loved ones entirely on my own shoulders. God can and does lift the burden, if I but let Him.

As I pray before the day starts, I may mention certain problems or situations in which I will need help during the day. I let God take them over. Then, relaxed and free from tension or worry, I go about the business of the day. And often I find that the situations I have dreaded do not materialize.

In the evening, before I go to sleep, I say thank You to God for His help during the day. If there are new needs I mention them in prayer. I ask for His armor of protection to surround my loved ones; I ask for His healing love to be poured out where it is needed; I ask for His abundance to come forth into every life.

As I do this day after day I truly learn to let go and let God.

My yoke is easy, and my burden is light.—Matthew 11:30

I now let go and let God.

DECEMBER 31, 1958

I am unfettered and unbound by past conditions and past circumstances. I bless all the wonderful days of this past year and I go forward into the new year, open and receptive to the good that God has in store for me.

In my oneness with God I release all thought of sickness or imperfection. I am ready for new life. I release all thought of hate or hurt. I am ready for a new understanding of people and conditions. I release all thought of poor financial conditions. I am ready for a new outpouring of substance. I release all thought of myself as bound by environment, heritage, education, or race. I am ready for a great spiritual growth.

I now let go and I let God go before me as I step over the threshold of the new year. I do not look back with self-recrimination or with longing to remain in the past. I know that all that has gone before has prepared me for the new growth that I am now ready to accept. I now let go and let God's Spirit in me act as a mighty magnet to attract my good to me.

Thou wilt keep him in perfect peace, whose mind is stayed on thee.—Isaiah 26:3

I let go and let God.

AUGUST 29, 1961

Let go and let God. "Let" is a small word but an important and meaningful one. When we let the Spirit of God work in and through our life, we are productive, successful, healthy, joyful, and enthusiastic.

Sometimes we feel that we need to insist on having our way. We feel that we need to compel or will things to happen. The sure way to our good is to let go and let God. Let go of negative thoughts and feelings. Let go of doubt, anxiety, and fear. Let go of limiting beliefs. Let go of all that is not in keeping with God.

The Spirit of God is complete and perfect within us. Wisdom is within us. Life is within us. Joy is within us. Love is within us. Peace, poise, and power are within us. All the attributes and qualities of God are within us. They come forth into our experience as we let God's Spirit work in and through us.

When we let go and let God, we let go of all that is not in keeping with God. We let God have His way in our mind, body, and affairs.

It is God who worketh in you both to will and to work, for his good pleasure.—Philippians 2:13

I let go. I let God.

MAY 30, 1968

Often the greatest help we receive comes through affirming the simplest of words, such as: "I let go. I let God." Yet nothing is more important to our personal, spiritual freedom than letting go and letting God. Letting go our fears lifts us in faith; letting go our needs and letting God show us the way of fulfillment brings forth blessings in our lives.

We need to remember that God does not do things for us, but God acts through us. God acts through us as we let go the lesser, as we let His presence and power work through us. When we let God's life be in charge of our body temple, it functions perfectly. When we let God's substance be active in us, our life prospers in creative, productive ways. As we let God's love take hold of our emotional nature, we are able to relate to others harmoniously and happily.

By letting go and letting God, we release our tense hold on things and allow room for the life, substance, and love of God to work through us and our affairs.

The branch cannot bear fruit by itself.—John 15:4

Chapel Flowers

Ruth Laurene

Tall white tapers light the room
Where I commune with Thee;
Lovely lilies breathe perfume
Where sadness used to be.

Blossoms from my old despair,
Bright beauty from my pain,
Radiance from selfless prayer—
These wondrous things remain,

Making beautiful the place
Of worship set apart,
Lending loveliness to grace
The chapel of my heart.

I let go and let God.

MAY 13, 1971

The phrase, "Let go and let God," is sometimes uttered without real thought or feeling. The mind often builds up an insulation against the overfamiliar. One way to keep such a phrase meaningful is to look at it as though seeing it for the first time. What does it really mean to let go and let God?

As we consider this statement, "Let go and let God," we should pay particular attention to the word *let*. It has only three letters, but its importance and significance in our lives cannot be overestimated. The word *let* indicates an attitude of mind, an attitude of assent, cooperation, consent. The word *let* both affirms and denies. We must let go the limiting thoughts which bind us to old conditions. There must be a willingness to let them go. Next must come the willingness to let the good flow in.

We can experience the sweeping freedom of the statement, "Let go and let God," as we apply it, with a new understanding of what it really means, to whatever situation may be confronting us.

Therefore we must pay the closer attention to what we have heard, lest we drift away from it.—Hebrews 2:1

I let go and let God.

MARCH 20, 1978

What do we let go, when we let go and let God? Certainly, we let fear go, we let anxiety go, we let feelings of impatience go. We let go any tendency to belittle or depreciate ourselves or to downgrade our abilities. We let go the habit of saying, "I can't," and hold to the realization that through the power of God in us, we can.

If we have been upset or unhappy because of the words or actions of another person, we let go and let God by letting love take the place of these feelings. If we have criticized or blamed another person, we let go and let God as we let forgiveness fill our heart and a new spirit of praise and appreciation be expressed through us.

When we let go and let God, we let go the negative and we stress and implement the positive.

Today, if any unwanted thoughts or feelings try to take over, let us calmly and quietly let go and let God—the Spirit of peace, the Spirit of love, the Spirit of faith, the Spirit of good—take over in us and in all that concerns us.

In thee my soul takes refuge.—Psalm 57:1

I relax, I let go, I let God do
his perfect work through me.

MAY 21, 1980

Sometimes we may come to the place where we do not know what to do or which way to turn. We may feel burdened by the thought that the solving of some problem or situation is all up to us.

When we depend on our personal powers alone, we may not feel equal to the problems that life poses. We need to remember that beyond our personal powers and capabilities is the spiritual power that is ours from God.

It is a great relief to realize that it is not all up to us, that God is the one presence and one power, ever working through us and through all that concerns us to adjust, to bless, to make all things right.

We are kept in perfect peace in mind and body as we give over our doubts and fears to God, as we let go and let Him do His perfect work through us. All is working out in perfect ways for all concerned.

I do not speak on my own authority; but the Father
who dwells in me does his works.—John 14:10

I let go and let God.

APRIL 22, 1988

Whenever I feel that the pressures of life are demanding more of me than I can give or more of me than I know how to give, I focus on the thought: I let go and let God. These words denote my positive approach to life. To affirm "I let go and let God" does not mean that I am willing to drift along and take whatever comes. To affirm "I let go and let God" is to be responsive to the power of the Almighty. I let go doubt and fear. I cooperate with the strong, vital, powerful spirit of God within me.

I let go and let God. I live a life of joy and enthusiasm as I eagerly move forward in life. I grow and unfold spiritually. I know that God is the one power in the universe, the one power active in me, the one power active in my life and affairs, the one power active in the lives of my dear ones.

I let go and let God. All is well concerning me, my dear ones, and my world.

Cast all your anxieties on him, for he cares about you.
—1 Peter 5:7

I let go and let God.

JANUARY 7, 1993

If you ever let thoughts of weakness, illness, or limitation in the front door of your mind, let them pass out the back door quickly. *Let go and let God.*

Let go. If negative thoughts are allowed to linger, they can become charged with emotion and embedded so that they close out good thoughts. How much better it is to let go unwanted thoughts and experiences.

Let God. Your mind is a fit setting for thoughts of wonder and appreciation for all the beauty in the world and for all the good that God is bringing forth into your life, body, and affairs.

Let go and let God. Your peaceful mind is your meeting ground with God. How precious are those moments of sweet communion. By letting go and letting God, you can keep this ground holy.

Fear not, for I am with you and will bless you.
—Genesis 26:24

As I let go and let God, I use the power to bless.

JULY 25, 1998

If my plan for peace of mind is simply letting go of worry, I may feel that I am giving up—on a goal, on myself, or on another person. However, an assurance of peace washes over me when I let go and then let God be God in my life and in the lives of my loved ones.

Just how do I do this? I let go of worry and then imagine myself giving the challenge or situation to God for the right solution. I take nothing back that I have given to God.

Letting go and letting God, I am doing something that has the power and potential to help me and to help others. So I can think clearly and act compassionately. I have a positive, uplifting attitude, and the people around me welcome my encouragement and support.

Then whoever invokes a blessing in the land shall bless by the God of faithfulness.—Isaiah 65:16

From the Readers of Daily Word

I would not be able to start my day properly without first reading the Daily Word. *My day goes better because of it.*

—R.W., BUFFALO, NEW YORK

My mom introduced me to Daily Word *and I know my daughter reads it and pray she instills to her daughters. My husband and I read it daily.*

—G.B., REEDLEY, CALIFORNIA

Letting go and letting God,
I am blessed and I bless others.

OCTOBER 16, 2001

Even though I care greatly about the health and well-being of a person or the outcome of a situation, I am careful not to let my caring turn into ongoing concern. Caring thoughts initiate action on my part, and I certainly pray for the person and about the situation.

In prayer, I let go of concern and turn in faith to God for the healing that is needed or the outcome that is best for everyone. Letting go and letting God, I release all to the One from whom healing and all other blessings flow.

I care about my loved ones and friends, about my home and job, about the world and the environment. Letting go of concern and placing all in the sacred realm of God's care, I am blessed and I also bless others.

Martha said to Jesus ... "Even now I know that God will give you whatever you ask of him." Jesus said to her, "Your brother will rise again."—John 11:21-23

My spirit soars as I let go and trust God.

NOVEMBER 9, 2009

As I step out in faith to do something new and daring, I may feel like a skydiver moments before a jump. When I make the conscious choice to let go of my comfortable surroundings, I may experience a moment of fear. But like the skydiver, my fear is quickly replaced with exhilaration and excitement as I soar through the experience with complete trust. I let go of my fear. God is with me and all is well!

Letting go of fear is liberating. As I let go and trust God, I open the way for God's perfect expression within me and in all the circumstances of my life. I don't worry about the outcome, for I know that all is well. I know that God is in charge and that I am being divinely guided and blessed.

Trust in the Lord forever.—Isaiah 26:4

I let go and let God steer me toward my highest good.

JULY 3, 2012

Everyone encounters bumps along the road of life. My response determines how smoothly I will navigate through any challenge.

I effortlessly yield to Spirit's guidance as I spend time in the sweetness of stillness. I release any burden of worry or strife and turn all concerns over to God.

Letting go and letting God is not abdicating my free will. It is an act of faith, of surrender. I use my free will to align with Divine Will, which is always for my highest good.

Regardless of where I am on my spiritual path, as I let go and let God, obstacles are eliminated. *I let go and let God steer me toward my highest good.*

And those who know your name put their trust in you.
—Psalm 9:10

I let go of fear and embrace love.

NOVEMBER 14, 2018

Because God's presence is in all things, everything that happens in my life occurs within divine order. I can let go of worry and fear because I trust the Divine within. If I am afraid, I may find myself in a state of unbelief, wanting to be in control. But when I let go of fear, I let go of stress and tension and can enjoy my life more.

I notice and let go of negative, fearful thoughts then fill that void with God thoughts. I use words of affirmation to assist me in fixing my mind on faith. As I change my mind, I shift away from stress and anxiety and into a state of peace. My entire body relaxes, and I know and trust that all is well. From this place of calm, I respond to life with ease and grace.

For I am convinced that neither death, nor life ...
will be able to separate us from the love of God in
Christ Jesus our Lord.—Romans 8:38, 39

I am peaceful and calm as I let go and let God.

NOVEMBER 6, 2020

When something is beyond my control or I'm facing a challenge and don't know what to do, the most productive thing I can do is let it go. I might write down my thoughts and then tear up the paper. Better still, I can take a moment to mentally step away by turning to God within.

I concentrate on my breathing and my heartbeat as I feel my oneness with God. In this sacred connection I release all. I envision any problem floating away on a breeze. In this moment, I let go of anxiety. I discover renewed hope and peace rising within my soul.

I continue to let go and let God whenever negative thoughts come to mind. I relax, giving thanks for grace and goodness in all its forms.

We know that all things work together for good for those who love God, who are called according to his purpose.
—Romans 8:28

Chapter 9

Messages of
DIVINE ORDER

Messages of
DIVINE ORDER

Just as we witness perfect patterns in nature, we humans live within God's pattern for our lives, called principles or Truth. As a species, we have only begun to understand what these principles are and how to use them, but we know divine order undergirds them. Through the years, *Daily Word* messages have told us we must first put our minds in order if we are to achieve harmony in our lives. An elevated consciousness aligns us with the perfect pattern of good established by principle.

Living in the Spirit of Renewal

By Michael Bernard Beckwith

MARCH/APRIL 2018

Just as the spring season consummates Mother Nature's evolutionary process, so do we evolve in sync with its dance, perfecting the creative energies we have been nurturing throughout earlier seasons of our lives, which are now ready to blossom into expression in, as, and through us. The question is: How can we best prepare ourselves for this next evolutionary leap?

The beautiful thing about the spiritual evolutionary process is that it takes place right on the altar of your own being—just you and your higher self, communing as one. In that sacred union, you enter a profound state of contentment, clarity, and receptivity. By anchoring yourself in such an affirmative state of consciousness, you empower yourself to enter the undiscovered regions of your being and blossom into more of your true self. In my own experience, I have identified specific spiritual practices that place me within hearing range of Spirit's gracious invitation into renewal.

It is through the practice of meditation that we learn to pay attention to reality, resulting in a realization of our oneness with Source.

There is no substitute for this divine communion, so if you haven't yet found a meditation practice, I encourage you to do your research and select a technique that suits your nature and include it in your daily routine.

Once we have tangibly tasted our oneness with Source, we become willing to surrender to its ongoing guidance and vision for our lives.

Surrender requires our readiness, commitment, patience, and the intentionality wherein we say to ourselves, *I am on the threshold of a deepening state of consciousness, a new state of being, and I surrender to every aspect of its unfoldment.* Through daily affirmative prayer we offer encouragement to ourselves, amplifying our intention to evolve and grow. [We] catch Spirit's vision for our lives, thus contributing to cocreating our lives and the unfoldment of our souls directly with Spirit.

We have now arrived at the outer blossoming of renewal, which is about putting into action our insights and how we are meant to deliver our gifts, talents, and skills as a beneficial presence on the planet. This aspect of renewal offers the opportunity to expand from a "me and mine" mindset into a "we" consciousness, impacting every community in which we are involved—family, the workplace, our spiritual community, neighborhood, town, state, the world.

There is no question that we are living in stressful, uncertain times, wherein a renewal of purpose and intention are vital to the creation of a society that honors the dignity of all beings. As I'm known to say, "The news informs us of what to include on our prayer list." As we relate to our world citizenship, I invite us not to allow fear to take over our hearts. Instead, let us turn within to our own true nature and trust in the grace that interpenetrates and surrounds all beings, thus renewing on the soul level our covenant with Spirit, ourselves, and all existence. As the realization that we are members of a global family finds its home in more and more hearts, it announces that now is the season to become a spiritual evolutionary who realizes that the solution to life's challenges is a spiritual one, that only victory through love is permanent.

Our affirmative response to Spirit's clarion call to recognize and honor our interconnectivity as one world family is a vital aspect of spiritual renewal. It is an acknowledgment that we have shaken off our winter sleep and have now awakened to the verdant, luscious, fertile, beautiful inner landscape within all beings as we go forward united as one global heart, together beaming a cosmic smile across the universe.

Michael Bernard Beckwith is the founder of Agape International Spiritual Center and has authored four award-winning books, including *Life Visioning* and *Spiritual Liberation*. Visit *agapelive.com* and *michaelbeckwith.com*.

Teach Me, Lord!

James Dillet Freeman

God, give me first a thirst to learn.
I pray the hours in which I turn
To books may be a happy time;
Make study seem my natural clime.

Give me delight in diligence,
Much common, some uncommon sense,
An ordered mind to get things straight,
And language to communicate;

God, I would have the faith to face
My unknown world of inner space
And find that if I dare try, I
May with no wings but winged thought fly!

And find what joy it is to be
One of the splendid company
Who undertake the undefined
Adventure of the human mind.

The perfect order of God is now manifest in all my affairs, and they are orderly and harmonious.

APRIL 23, 1926

Our speaking the word of authority to our affairs causes them to become orderly and harmonious. Very often the reason why one fails to realize prosperity is that his mind and his affairs are not in order. Declaring order, we set our affairs aright; we cause them to be divinely adjusted and to become perfectly harmonious.

When we place our affairs in order, anyone or anything which is related to them comes into harmonious adjustment. Nothing escapes the power of our word. The adjusting power of Spirit is not completed until its work is perfect and is entirely satisfactory to our well-being.

Without perfect order the planets of the universe would clash. Without such order, the sun and the moon would be disorderly in their movements. In God's universe perfect order must be maintained at all times.

When one is in the consciousness of order, nothing disorderly can find place in him or in his affairs. It would seem that all things in his life move with perfect ease to respect the orderliness of his consciousness. Everything comes just at the right time and in the right manner.

Order is heaven's first law.—Pope

The adjusting power of Spirit regulates all my affairs.
The very order of heaven is now manifest in the earth.

APRIL 3, 1928

The confusion which sometimes appears in one's life or in his affairs results from a confusion of ideas. When one is confused in his thought, he causes confusion about him.

The remedy for confusion lies in a consciousness of perfect order. One needs to take his mind right off disorder and confusion. He needs to break all relation with disorderly conditions. He should think of himself as dwelling in a place where perfect order reigns just as he would be doing were he, at the present time, living in a state of perfect peace.

When one's mind becomes orderly in its deliberations it becomes a vehicle which Spirit uses in causing perfect order to appear. The regulating and adjusting power of divine mind working through the mind of man brings about perfect order.

When one's affairs are in a disorderly condition, he should first become orderly in mind. His affairs are so closely connected with his thought that his thought of order will speedily manifest in his affairs. At no time should he permit himself to become mentally connected with the disorder which appears.

Let all things be done decently and in order.
—1 Corinthians 14:40

The very order of heaven is now manifest in my mind and in my affairs, and all my world is in order.

MAY 28, 1931

The orderly nature of the universe is, indeed, an example for us in the matter of orderliness. As we gaze upon the perfect order of all things in God's universe, we are prompted to put our own affairs in order, to see divine order manifest in our everyday world.

Disorder may be traced back to a measure of disorderliness in mind. When there is evidence of disorder in our affairs, we need to become more orderly in our thinking. We need to establish mental poise and to become conscious masters over our thoughts instead of letting them run riot without supervision.

Order, then, comes as a result of consciousness of order. If things in our world seem to be disorderly we need first to make the adjustment in mind. We must be poised in mind, have orderly thoughts, have the consciousness of perfect order in Spirit, before trying to arrange outer things in order.

There is always a bit of heaven coming into evidence when we place our affairs in order. They seem to come under the management of heaven when we seek to express its order.

That thou shouldest set in order the things that were wanting.—Titus 1:5

*God's will for me is divine order
in my mind, body, and affairs.*

JANUARY 23, 1939

Unless you grew up in Truth, you probably remember a time when you thought the phrase "divine order" meant a sort of divine discipline. Now that you live by the higher law, however, all this is changed. Unhappiness and inharmony are never in divine order. God's law of love entails no hardship for you; on the contrary, it includes all the good that you can ever need or desire.

When you try to establish yourself in perfect health you are working with divine order. When you give your associates your utmost in good will and co-operation you are an aid to another phase of divine order. When you come into the understanding of God's bounty and so enjoy real prosperity, you are helping divine order to prevail. When you put off the finite and put on the Christ perfection even as Jesus did, divine order will always prevail so far as you are concerned.

Behold now, I have set my cause in order.—Job 13:18

Divine order is established in my mind,
in my heart, and in all of my affairs.

JUNE 24, 1946

Time and energy that could be more constructively employed are sometimes taken up in straightening out a disorderly state of affairs caused by a state of disorder in your mind and heart. Order in your thoughts and actions brings peace and serenity to your mind and smoothness and ease in every detail of your affairs.

Begin each day by acknowledging that the spirit of divine order is established in your mind and affairs. As you organize your plans for the day, allow time for each task to be completed in order, and make it your custom to be punctual in keeping all appointments. If something happens that seems upsetting, become quiet for a moment and reaffirm your oneness with divine order. As you do this you will regain your poise, and you will be able to turn discord into harmony, confusion into peace. Establishing orderly habits in the smallest details of your life will identify you with universal order and harmony, and all your affairs will become peaceful and harmonious.

I have given thee a wise and an understanding heart.
—1 Kings 3:12

My thinking is in tune with God,
and my life is blessed with divine order.

DECEMBER 26, 1947

There is a basic order in the universe that is apparent to us as we observe the precision of planetary action and other movements in nature. There is a basic order in our individual world too though it may not always be apparent.

The way to realize this basic order in our life is to think in tune with God. Instead of thinking of disease and weakness we need to think of health and strength. Instead of thinking of lack and limitation we need to think of plenty and power. Instead of thinking of what other persons should be doing for us we need to think of what we should be doing for ourselves. Instead of thinking of old age and death we need to think of energy and life. Instead of thinking of ourselves in the light of our past experiences we need to think of ourselves in the light of the creativeness of our spiritual powers.

Through our thinking we create either order or disorder in our life. We are the masters.

In the morning shalt thou hear my voice;
In the morning will I order my prayer.—Psalm 5:3

From the Readers of Daily Word

Daily Word *gives inspiration each day from a reservoir of peace and love.*

— M.S., WALTHAM, MASSACHUSETTS

I treasure Daily Word *devotional. I have been reading this devotional for more than 60 years (since teenage years). Especially grateful for the large print as I am now in the late 70s.*

— B.H., LOXAHATCHEE, FLORIDA

Daily Word *has been my bedside companion/inspiration for 35 years. I feel lost without it. I am grateful.*

— P.A., JEFFERSON CITY, MISSOURI

Divine order and harmony are now established in my mind, body, and affairs through the power of the indwelling Christ.

JANUARY 8, 1950

Most of us feel a need for greater order in some phase of our life. We may need order in the functioning of the organs of our body; we may need order in our diet, balance in the selection of our food. We may need order in our environment; we may need order in our relations with our fellow men. We may need more wisdom and good judgment in handling our money, more discretion in our spending and saving. We may need order in our mind. We may need to learn to concentrate, to use our powers intelligently, to avoid scattering our forces by worry and fear.

Whatever our need for order, the answer lies in the realization that the very Spirit of life and wisdom and supply is within us, the Spirit of the indwelling Christ. Let us affirm that divine order and harmony are now established in our mind, body, and affairs.

I can do all things in him that strengtheneth me.
—Philippians 4:13

I am quickened into an understanding of my part in establishing divine order in my world.

JANUARY 9, 1959

Whenever anything goes wrong in my life it is an indication that there is something in me that needs to be met. At such a time I ask the Father within me to show me what it is that I need to do to make things right in order to establish divine order.

If I have been prone to blame some person or some situation for the problem I face, I now let go any such thought. It is possible that the other person has some responsibility toward harmonizing the problem; it is possible that the situation is not of my creating. But, when my own attitude is right, when I am loving, trusting, and nonresistant, I am able to handle the problem wisely and dissolve the inharmony quickly.

It is through prayer that I am enabled to change my attitude. It is through prayer that I am quickened into an understanding of my part in establishing divine order. It is through prayer that I am given the willing spirit that is needed to make any overcoming.

Praying at all seasons in the Spirit.—Ephesians 6:18

Divine order is now established in my mind, body, and affairs through the power of the indwelling Christ.

AUGUST 28, 1963

What does divine order mean? It means a right relationship of things, a balance, an orderly outworking of our affairs. Divine order begins within us. It begins as we establish a right relationship with God. When we are attuned to God, when we know and feel our oneness with Him, then everything in our outer life falls into place, following the perfect pattern of good that is God's will for us.

If there seems to be confusion in our mind or affairs, if our life seems hurried or cluttered, we need to stop and declare divine order. We need to establish ourselves in divine order through the quietness of prayer. As we are balanced and poised in the Christ Mind, we approach everything in our life differently. We see ways to set things right. We are led to take the action that will bring order. We are inspired with the vision to discern between the essential and the nonessential. We are free to devote our time and energy to the things that really matter.

Let all things be done ... in order.—1 Corinthians 14:40

I stand firm in the faith that the light of God inspires me to live in divine order.

APRIL 7, 1967

The little boy was busily picking up his toys and placing them in the gaily covered box he kept them in. He had learned that he must do first things first, that he was able to and was expected to put his room in order.

We all need to learn to do first things first. We all need to put ourselves in order. There is a divine order for our mind, our body, and our affairs, but sometimes even as we pray for divine order we neglect doing first things first. We seem to want to skip over the untidy issues of life and let them take care of themselves.

If we are to live in divine order we must take the steps we can take in order to ready ourselves. A prayer for inspiration and guidance gives us the light to see what we should be doing so that, like the little boy, we are able to put our "room" in order. Then we can go happily about the adventure of living, knowing that we have done what we can do and what we are expected to do.

If any of you lacks wisdom, let him ask God who gives to all men generously.—James 1:5

The Origin

Yaisha Vargas

And God removed all standing points.
And God took away all mirrors.
And there was nothing left,
but God ...

And while falling in God there was
the vastness of the silent Allness,
a stillness suspended in ecstasy,
the Idea of a pulsating Universe
in the sparkling womb of a grain of sand,
the Silence that howled,
birthing its raging Force across Totality ...

And then ...

There was a witness, a poet,
Who made sense of it All.
She weaved the thought of the first stanza
and sang the first word of a song—
a vibration that swirled on itself,
and whirled
and turned
into a soul.

God's order is the foundation for divine order in my life.

APRIL 17, 1973

What if at this moment every person in the world decided to bring himself or herself into divine order? What if every person made a valiant effort to put the house of his heart, the house of his mind, the house he calls home, the house of his world in divine order? Can you envision the changes that would take place?

This what-if is an exercise in picturization in which we can all participate. As we do our part, as we pray to make the changes that divine order requires, we gain the poise, the patience, the awareness needed. We build upon the faith that God's order is foundation for divine order in our lives.

God is light, so when all is in order, all is illumined. God is life, so when all is in order, there is only health and perfection. God is substance, so when all is in order, there is plenty to fulfill every need. God is peace, so when all is in order, all is harmonious. God is joy, so when all is in order, a song of hallelujah envelops earth.

Build up, build up, prepare the way.—Isaiah 57:14

God's law of good is operating in and through my life as divine order.

JULY 7, 1978

When there are needs in life, regardless of their nature it is good to pray a prayer for divine order. To pray for divine order is to pray for the establishment of right and just and loving outcomes. Our prayer for divine order enables us to gain a proper perspective of every situation and to see God's law of good at work.

We can affirm divine order knowing that it encompasses all kinds of needs. Healing is in divine order, prosperity is in divine order, guidance is in divine order, protection is in divine order, harmony is in divine order. All the good we can ever imagine is in divine order, for God's law is good.

We open ourselves to divine order through our faith-filled prayers and through committing our lives, our plans, all that concerns us to God's law of good operating in and through us as divine order.

The law of the Lord is perfect, reviving the soul.
—Psalm 19:7

Through Christ in me divine order is made manifest in me and all that concerns me.

APRIL 2, 1982

If some situation seems confused and out of order, I affirm divine order. Though I may not see it when I look at surface appearances, there is a divine order underlying all things. I call this divine order forth by my steadfast trust in Christ, the source of divine order.

Divine order means that all things fall into place, that every needed adjustment is made, that every good desire is fulfilled, at the right time, in the right way.

Divine order means that my body is healthy, that every part functions perfectly, that I have the strength to do the things before me this day.

Divine order means peace of mind and freedom from unhappy thinking; it means inner control, inner confidence and courage.

Through Christ in me divine order is made manifest in me and in all that concerns me.

The law of the Lord is perfect.—Psalm 19:7

Thoughts of divine order keep me on a path of order.

OCTOBER 13, 1987

Divine order is the reality of God's presence throughout all creation, governing its orderly and timely unfoldment. Nothing can interfere with an order that is divine in character. As I think thoughts of divine order, I prepare myself to recognize order and to align my life and affairs with it.

I am aware of my thoughts. I think orderly thoughts, and they go before me to prepare the way of order. My life and affairs are in order.

I am aware of the beauty of order in all creation. The unfailing order of the seasons and the patterns of growth that are so intricate and dependable constantly inspire me to keep my thoughts on divine order.

No event or person has the power to disturb or upset the order and stability of my life. My thoughts of divine order keep me on a path of order.

I am with you in spirit, rejoicing to see your good order and the firmness of your faith in Christ.—Colossians 2:5

Divine order and right outworkings are present and active in my life and affairs.

SEPTEMBER 11, 1991

When unexpected events happen, situations change, or conditions seem out of harmony, we may lose a sense of order in our lives. Divine order, however, is always present, even though we may not be aware of it.

When we adjust our thinking, we bring order back into focus. As we calm agitated feelings or stressful thoughts, we bring inner peace into outer expression.

Let us affirm: *Divine order and right outworkings are present in my life and affairs.* This healthy activity will manifest itself outwardly as we continue to think thoughts of divine order. We envision the whole universe in order. We attune ourselves to the flow of divine order so that we do not impede any blessings. We assist the manifestation of order by incorporating orderliness in all that we think and do.

All things should be done decently and in order.
—1 Corinthians 14:40

I am living in the flow of divine order.

APRIL 30, 1998

I know there is a divine order always active in the universe, but do I always know that divine order is constant in my life?

I do when I stop relying on situations and circumstances for my hope. I do when I take a deep breath, become still, and draw on inner wisdom for my understanding, all of which open me to a world of order.

I begin to think and speak and act from the presence of God within me. Life takes on new purpose and meaning. It's as if I have stepped back in order to see the whole panoramic view of life and how I fit into the order of it all. I have found my way, and I no longer struggle, for I am caught up in the gentle, constant flow of divine order.

Thus says the Lord, who gives the sun for light by day and the fixed order of the moon and the stars for light by night.—Jeremiah 31:35

From the Readers of Daily Word

I enjoy each moment I live, then you'll really know the fullness of the blessing God can give to follow God's way. I love the Daily Word.

—S.W., ATLANTA, GEORGIA

Daily Word *gives me that push I need for the beginning of my day. It gives me peace.*

—E.T., ATLANTA, GEORGIA

I love my Daily Word. *I have been reading it now for 40 years. It makes me very joyful and I am blessed through it.*

—I.B., BUELLTON, CALIFORNIA

> *Divine order is actively at work in my life and in all creation.*

AUGUST 21, 2002

I do make plans for the future, and I act on them. But because I affirm that divine order is at work in my life and in all life, I don't worry about or question future events. They will unfold at the right time and in the right way. My responsibility is to connect with the divine order that is working in and through my life right now and then to cooperate with it. I learn from the past and plan for the future, but I live in the present.

Rather than trying to reason things out by myself, I rely on divine wisdom to guide me by trusting in the guidance I receive.

God's order is actively at work in my life and in all creation. I have faith in the guiding light of God that brings order into my life and into the world around me.

Seek the Lord and his strength; seek his presence continually. Remember the wonderful works he has done.—Psalm 105:4-5

*I am living in and from the divine order
of life every day.*

OCTOBER 25, 2005

There may be some aspects of myself that seem out of order or out of character for me. As I bring them into the light of Spirit, a transformation takes place and I see them in divine order.

When my thoughts are illumined by the light of Spirit, a transformation takes place: willfulness becomes willingness, judgmental thinking becomes good judgment, and vanity becomes healthy self-regard. A perception of neediness is revealed to be a desire that has become misdirected. As I release thoughts of lack, I open the door to the abundance of God.

Divine light dispels all doubt. I give thanks for divine light that shows me the good which is within me and directs me in expressing that good. All is in divine order.

*He reveals deep and hidden things; he knows what is in the
darkness, and light dwells with him.—Daniel 2:22*

Divine order prevails in my life, and I am grateful.

APRIL 10, 2013

When I face challenges, seeking advice from others may sometimes be confusing. Rather than look elsewhere, I remember to trust in divine order. As I enter a sacred time of prayer, divine order prevails. Resistant or rebellious thoughts become quiet, and in the stillness, I open to divine wisdom.

Confusion falls away as I acknowledge God's infinite intelligence. The mind of God holds a solution to every problem. I am one with Divine Mind. As I become still and receptive, ideas surface and I feel a rush of energy. I prepare to take inspired action.

When I put God first, divine order prevails in my life, and I am grateful.

When a land rebels it has many rulers; but with an intelligent ruler there is lasting order.—Proverbs 28:2

I gratefully surrender to the spiritual certainty that my life is in divine order.

NOVEMBER 5, 2017

The idea of *surrender* can feel alarming to my limited, mortal mind and seemingly synonymous with defeat. In Truth, however, surrender is an essential spiritual step that allows divine order to guide every choice and challenge in my life.

Divine order is the essence of all life, the infinite love in which I "live and move and have my being" (Acts 17:28). Divine order is always present and always expressing. So any perceived absence of order tells me that I am allowing my mortal mind to stray from the loving guidance of my spiritual Self.

Divine order is my choice. I exchange fear-based priorities and expectations for the Presence within—my constant, loving guide to a life of joy and peace.

For surely I know the plans I have for you ... to give you a future with hope.—Jeremiah 29:11

Divine order is a blessing in my life.

JANUARY 25, 2022

Unity poet James Dillet Freeman once said that no prayer is as powerful as simply affirming divine order. The beauty of this prayer is that it doesn't call for a specific result but instead affirms that everything is unfolding according to a divine pattern. The manifestations of this prayer may seem miraculous, but they are actually perfect demonstrations of spiritual law.

Divine order brings harmony to my life and to the world. Just as I trust the sun to rise and set daily, so, too, I trust divine order to support every aspect of life—seen and unseen, known and unknown. I affirm divine order and rest assured that infallible, unchanging spiritual law is, always and forever, in and through all things.

For surely I know the plans I have for you, says the Lord, plans for your welfare and not for harm, to give you a future with hope.—Jeremiah 29:11

Chapter 10

Messages of PEACE

Messages of
PEACE

For 100 years, *Daily Word* has been reminding its readers there is a place deep within us where we can find the peace that surpasses understanding. It is the Divine in us, the Christ energy that animates our human existence. Here, peace on earth begins. These messages remind us that when we find peace for ourselves, we help bring about peace for the rest of the world through our thoughts and actions.

Toward a Peace with Justice

By Robert H. Frowick

JULY 2005

On countless occasions when I was having dinner by myself someplace in the Balkans or elsewhere in Europe, I would take a photo of my beautiful wife out of my wallet and put it up against the candle on the table as if I were having dinner with her. Then I felt some comfort from the loneliness of being away from Ann and our children.

I had retired from the U.S. Foreign Service with the personal rank of Ambassador in 1989. We were living in California when I received a call to help bring peace and democracy to the Balkans. Not being with my family was the hardest part of my assignments there.

The political map of Europe changed fundamentally in 1989 and 1990: Soviet power collapsed; Germany was peacefully reunited; and all the countries of Eastern Europe started regaining their independence. In the former Soviet Union and Yugoslav Federation, tensions over ethnic differences had been bottled up for a long time under Communism. Then ethnic differences began to reassert themselves, creating enormous political strains in both places.

A Changing World

I was repeatedly called out of retirement to deal with the Balkan problems related to the explosive decompression of Yugoslavia. Wars of "ethnic cleansing" were sweeping across one part after another of Yugoslavia. A way to restore peace and establish justice was desperately needed.

In October 1995, I was asked to serve as initial Head of Mission for the Organization for Security and Cooperation in Europe

(OSCE) in postwar Bosnia and Herzegovina. OSCE includes all the countries of Europe plus the United States and Canada. The Dayton Peace Agreement ending the war in Bosnia called on the OSCE to supervise elections, stimulate democratization, and oversee the dismantling of weapons.

But there was no blueprint for action. Ours was a pioneering mission. I had no instructions from Washington or the OSCE. So I studied the Dayton Agreement and just tried to think my way through with common sense as to how to meet the challenges we were facing.

The Right Guidance

Reading *Daily Word* magazine, I found the energy, strength, and faith to carry out the tasks required of us. Day in and day out for the more than two years I spent in Bosnia, I would start my day reading *Daily Word* and being guided to do what was right.

At each stage I tried to determine the best strategies to reach our goals and how I could muster the strength to get through the whole thing. *Daily Word* was absolutely critical in helping me do that. My wife would always find a way to mail *Daily Word* to me. Sometimes it was a bit late, and when that happened, I would go back and read the days of the previous month so I would have something to keep me going.

Before walking into a difficult, uncertain negotiating session, I would spend time in prayer. Often just before going into such meetings, I would touch the *Daily Word,* which was always in my pocket. I was trying to be an agent of God. When colleagues sometimes said I was "doing the Lord's work," I thought they could not know how true that was.

Peace and Justice

January 1, 1996, marked the beginning of peace in Bosnia. On that day I asked myself, *What can I best do to start the year?* I decided to meet with the religious leaders: the head of the Muslim faith, the Roman Catholic Cardinal, and the local Serbian Orthodox priest. In each case I said: "We now have a political settlement. Will you begin to preach forgiveness? If you can't forget the war, can't you at least forgive and establish contacts again with one another's religious leadership to develop a dialogue and work toward reconciliation?"

I stayed long enough to witness some of that reconciliation and the building of a democratic process. On election day in 1996, more than 100,000 people were involved in helping voters establish a democratic structure of government. In 1996 and 1997, OSCE supervised elections for all levels of government, built up the country's biggest human rights and democratization program, and oversaw the destruction of more than 6,500 armaments. That's when I knew it was time to come home to my family.

Someone once said to me, "Bob, a man's two most important decisions are choosing a professional career and choosing his partner for life." I feel unbelievably blessed on both counts and deeply appreciate the guidance given to me by *Daily Word*.

Robert Frowick retired from the U.S. Foreign Service in 1989. Among his roles, he has served as special adviser to the State Department for Balkan elections. Residing in Santa Rosa, California, he and his wife of 28 years have brought up six children. Robert enjoys golf but wonders if he will ever be completely retired.

[Update: Frowick died in 2007 at age 77. "He was the finest diplomat I've ever met and, frankly, the finest human being I've ever met, or will meet," David Foley, a State Department spokesman, told the *Washington Post*. "He had amazing skills to get people to trust him, to believe him and to make compromises they wouldn't make for anyone else."]

Shift and Lift

Kalila Volkov

Choosing to escape chaos
We can release ourselves to quiet
And surrender to the ocean of breath,
Joy and gratitude ablaze in our hearts.
As we remember to trust divine wisdom
We take a step into paradise
And linger where all is comfort.

Resting in awareness
Of soul wholeness
We can soak in the power of positivity
And bathe in a galaxy of peace,
Letting our gifts of blessings pour out.

May we all attune to our gentle inner teacher,
Dipping into Spirit's well of serenity.
Let's connect with our centers and each other,
With the true sight of nonjudgment,
And restore an undivided brotherhood.

*The peace of God fills my heart
and I am at peace with all things.*

APRIL 19, 1927

The peace of God sets me free from all tendency to be inharmonious, worried, and irritable. This peace pervades my consciousness and gives me peaceful thoughts. I exchange inharmonious thoughts for thoughts of harmony and peace.

My heart is filled with the abundance of God's peace. I feel at peace with all persons and all things. Everyone whom I contact senses this peace and, in turn, is lifted to the holy peace and quietness of Spirit.

I am at peace with the past. All memory of wrongs is wiped from my consciousness and I am at peace with past events. I am pacified and reconciled to the holy peace of God.

I am at peace with my environment. Nothing can disturb the calm peace of my soul. My inner peace extends to the very circumference of my environment.

I am at peace with life. I find no disappointments in life. I do not resist the circumstances which take place in my affairs.

My heart overflows with peace. I see myself and my whole world established in the peace of God which passes all human understanding.

Let the peace of Christ rule in your hearts.—Colossians 3:15

I abide in the perfect peace which comes through having the mind freed from all burdens and established in divine harmony.

NOVEMBER 11, 1927

My mind is relieved from all mental tension and all sense of depression and bondage. My mind is freed from tense conditions, charged with new ideas and with refreshing thoughts. I am freed from depression, and I realize that I am under no adverse thought. I am mentally free and relieved of all sense of burden.

I am established in perfect peace and in divine harmony, and I am at peace with all my fellows. I will permit no inharmonious thought to disturb this perfect peace. I refuse to believe anything which would tend to disrupt peace or to make me antagonistic.

I resolve to do my part toward establishing universal peace. I will be peaceful in my home and at my work. I will try to bring about peace in every situation in which hatred or antagonism becomes evident. Divine harmony now prevails in every part of my being.

They shall beat their swords into plowshares, and their spears into pruning-hooks; nation shall not lift up sword against nation, neither shall they learn war any more.—Micah 4:3

Every disturbing element is removed from my world because my mind is ruled and pervaded by infinite peace.

JANUARY 8, 1930

When we are established in the peace of God, inharmony and disorder have no place in our life. When we realize our oneness with infinite peace, we live in a world in which there are no disturbing elements.

If you would have a peaceful world, be peaceful-minded. Drop from mind every thought that would disturb your peace of mind. Cast from mind every belief that would destroy your peace. Rest in the peace of Spirit and let your mind be pervaded with infinite peace.

Do not think of a peaceful world as an abnormal one. If noise and inharmony have filled your world, you may think of peace as too passive to be desirable. On the contrary, peace is natural to the spiritual man and as we lift our thought to God we find the world of peace to be the true world of Spirit.

Every peaceful thought that you think will contribute to your peace. Every slight realization of peace will help you to realize more clearly that peace is now yours—peace in mind, in body, and in environment.

Now the God of peace ... make you perfect in every good thing to do his will.—Hebrews 13:20, 21

The peace of God rules my mind and I am peaceful in all my relations with others.

DECEMBER 7, 1934

I am now at peace with myself, with God in the midst of me, and with all persons. I have found at the heart of my being the very presence of God, the presence of peace. I know that peace emanates from this presence to all parts of my world.

Since God as peace rules my mind, all my inharmonious thoughts are overcome. The peace of God rules my consciousness so thoroughly that no inharmonious thought can exist in my mind. This peace is akin to the peace of heaven. I know that Christ is now sharing His peace with me, and I become His agent to help establish peace on earth.

With peace in my mind, I am assured of peace in my body. My body is at peace because there are no disturbing thoughts in my mind. My peaceful attitude assures me of peace in my nerves, cells, and muscles. The parts of my body are at peace with each other and work together harmoniously.

God's peace is the peace that prevails throughout my organism. Every part of my world is filled with His peace.

Now the God of peace ... make you perfect in every good thing.—Hebrews 13:20

*As a radiating center of divine love and harmony
I am contributing to world peace.*

DECEMBER 5, 1940

Do you know that you can play an important part in establishing peace in the world? You need not be a statesman, a diplomat, a soldier, or a public speaker. Right where you are you can render a great service in the cause of peace.

Peace in its truest sense will not be secured by the victories of war, by arbitration, or by statesmanship. Lasting peace will come when ideas of peace, love, and good will prevail in the minds of men. When you are harmonious and loving in thought, word, and deed, you are consecrating the services of one more individual to the cause of peace. More than this, you are radiating peace and love to those about you, thereby helping them to be harmonious. They in turn will transmit the consciousness of peace to others. As an individual your power to promote peace is limitless. You will be working in unity of purpose with a vast army of consecrated persons throughout the world.

Blessed are the peacemakers.—Matthew 5:9

Peace on earth, good will toward men.

JULY 24, 1945

On the back of every envelope that goes out from Unity are these words: "Peace on earth, good will toward men." It is a continual reminder to us at Unity and to the countless thousands who receive mail from 917 Tracy, Kansas City, Missouri, to keep faithful in prayer for world peace. It is a reminder too of the angels' song of peace that hovered over the earth when Christ was born, the song that for two thousand years has been heard in human hearts and souls in spite of the wars waged in the world.

When you think about the world situation, when you long for universal peace among all men, take the time to give your blessing to the world. Affirm, "On earth peace, good will toward men." Have faith in the Spirit of God in man to inspire, to illumine, to act through him as good will, as peace. You cannot realize how important your prayers are, nor how far-reaching their effect. Even one person praying for peace projects a blessing into the world that adds to the goodwill consciousness that promotes peace among all people.

And on earth peace among men, in whom he is well pleased.—Luke 2:14

From the Readers of Daily Word

Daily Word *has been a rich treasure trove of inspiration to me and my friends for years! Words cannot express how much we value it. Grateful indeed.*

—J.Y., HOCKESSIN, DELAWARE

My mother has been a life subscriber and for years I was her one-year gift subscription receiver. She will turn 102 this coming May. I have been a subscriber for the last few years and plan to follow in her steps. I recently lost my husband of 56 years and Daily Word *provides comfort and meaning to my days.*

—E.I., SAN ANTONIO, TEXAS

I have faith in God; I have faith in his spirit in me and in my fellow men; I have faith in the unassailable structure of God's world. I am at peace.

NOVEMBER 11, 1952

On Armistice Day everyone's thought is centered on peace, and we all pray for lasting peace for all the peoples of the world.

Jesus said: "Peace I leave with you; my peace I give unto you: not as the world giveth, give I unto you. Let not your heart be troubled, neither let it be fearful."

Peace, then, is something we already have. Peace is something we must realize and accept rather than fight for. Peace accompanies faith and disappears with fear. "Let not your heart be troubled, neither let it be fearful."

Peace comes with faith. When a person has faith in God and faith in God's Spirit in himself and in his fellow men, when he has faith in the unassailable structure of God's world, then he has a deep and abiding peace. Then he is able to contribute to the peace of the world.

Peace I leave with you; my peace I give unto you ...
Let not your heart be troubled.—John 14:27

In the name of the Lord Jesus Christ we pray for and decree a permanent peace, uniting all the nations of the earth in a league of justice and righteousness, in which the life, liberty, and love of God shall be paramount.

MAY 1, 1955

This prayer for peace was given us by Charles Fillmore, cofounder of Unity. In Silent Unity we pray every day for world peace. We know that world peace can be brought about only when the individuals who make up the nations of the earth are quickened with God's Spirit of justice, love, wisdom, and light.

Every individual has an important contribution to make to the peace of the world. One important contribution all of us who read *Daily Word* and pray together can make is to give the substance of our thought and faith to praying for peace.

"Where two or three are gathered together in my name, there am I in the midst of them." We may be sure that as we pray together in the name of Jesus Christ for peace, His presence is with us, in the very midst of us, giving power and life to our prayers.

The earth is Jehovah's.—Psalm 24:1

Peace like a river flows into my mind and heart.

AUGUST 4, 1961

"Peace like a river, it floweth so free,
Out from the heart of infinity."

Let the thought of "peace like a river" fill your mind. Relax and let the feeling of peace, God's peace, flow through you. The peace that is perfect, the peace that is past understanding comes to you from the heart of infinity, which is God at the heart of you, God at the heart of all.

Nerves are quieted, muscles relax, tensions subside, emotions are calmed, minds become clear as peace possesses us. Jesus said, "Peace I leave with you; my peace I give unto you: not as the world giveth, give I unto you." The peace that is of the Spirit comes to us from the Prince of Peace, the living Christ. This is the peace that we have sought for and have not found in outer things.

Let us rest in the peace of Christ, let us let it flow over us and through us, a healing stream, a river of life. Let us say to ourselves whenever we feel unquiet or tense, "Peace like a river flows into my mind and heart."

Peace I leave with you; my peace I give unto you.
—John 14:27

I am a peacemaker.

APRIL 8, 1968

Jesus said, "Blessed are the peacemakers, for they shall be called sons of God." Every one of us can be a peacemaker. To be a peacemaker is more than just being peaceful; it is more than just passively agreeing with others in order not to cause argument; it is more than saying, "Peace, peace" when there is no peace.

To be a peacemaker means just what it says. It is to make peace; it is to do something about peace; it is to work with ourselves and with conditions, and with other people so that peace is brought forth.

All of us know people who are peacemakers, whose very presence brings peace to any gathering. We can all be this kind of person. We all know the kinds of words and actions that promote peace, just as we know the kinds of words and actions that stir up turmoil, that alienate people, that downgrade people.

We work on the side of peace; we become peacemakers as in our thoughts, words, and deeds we express our highest concept of peace.

Blessed are the peacemakers, for they shall be called sons of God.—Matthew 5:9

Harvest in the Heart

James Dillet Freeman

There is a harvest in the heart
That acres cannot yield;
The living spirit of a man
Is like a fertile field.
For faith is like a mustard seed,
How great its increment!
From every prayer of faith we reap
A harvest of content.

What tins and bins and granaries
Can hold the heart's increase,
The overflowing jubilance,
The heaped-up, pressed-down peace;
The riches of the spirit
Unfolding fruitfully,
Thought on thought and deed on deed
Into maturity!

My mind is at peace; my heart is at peace; my emotions are balanced and peaceful. I am at peace.

MAY 17, 1970

How fortunate is the person who, reading today's prayer thought, finds it in complete agreement with the state of his mind, heart, and emotions. To all who have a peaceful mind, a peaceful heart, peaceful emotions, we extend a special invitation to pour out a blessing on those who have a need for peace today.

There are saddened hearts, troubled hearts, fearful hearts. Yet within each person lies the possibility for peace. This peace is not passive acceptance of inharmony or unhappiness. This peace pervades the person, making him whole again. This peace brings balance to the emotions so that there is a harmonious handling of self and situations.

When we speak words of peace, as when we speak any positive word of prayer, we are coming into agreement with God's will for us. We are accepting the peace God has prepared. It is ready. Let us accept God's peace and be at peace.

I will make a covenant of peace with them.—Ezekiel 37:26

My heart is attuned to the universal spirit of peace.

FEBRUARY 6, 1977

If I have any tendency to fret about dissension in the world, I remember that God is the universal spirit of peace. Beneath the conflict of world affairs, the smooth tenor of God's plan for mankind prevails.

I keep my heart attuned to the universal spirit of peace. I make sure that my thoughts and actions foster justice and amity. As I achieve indwelling peace and poise, I am better able to understand others and to communicate the spirit of fellowship that I feel. I increase the harmony within my own personal sphere of activity as I express a spirit of love, faith, peace, and cooperation.

I know that my prayers combined with the prayers of others have an influence upon global peace. My mind is alert to every sign of the desire of others to share a new song of justice and unity and to establish peace on earth.

I will sing of loyalty and of justice ... I will walk with integrity of heart within my house.—Psalm 101:1, 2

> *The peace of God fills my mind and body, and I am healed.*

AUGUST 29, 1980

If I have a healing need, I relax in the knowledge that perfect health is my God-given birthright. God is my perfect health. I look past the appearance and call forth the perfection of God.

I open myself to perfect health by letting go all inharmonious thoughts and feelings. There is no room in my heart for unloving, unforgiving feelings. My peaceful thoughts free me to express perfect health.

Jesus said, "Peace I leave with you; my peace I give to you." I let the peace of God fill my mind and heart, harmonizing my thoughts and feelings. I speak words of peace to the cells of my body. I feel God's peace vitalizing and renewing me.

I affirm: *The peace of God fills my mind and body, and I am healed.* I rejoice, confident that I am being renewed and restored. I claim perfect health today.

Peace I leave with you; my peace I give to you.—John 14:27

I pray for peace throughout the world.

NOVEMBER 8, 1988

The peace within each person in the world is a beginning point of peace for the whole world.

In prayer I establish peace within myself. I still my racing thoughts and maintain a serene attitude of inner peace. I pray for wisdom to see and to experience harmony in all situations and relationships. I know that I walk in love and with God wherever I go.

I pray to see the child of God within each person I meet, and to know that a spirit of cooperation, love, and peace governs all people. I encourage peace wherever I am.

My prayer for peace includes all the people of the world. I pray for peace-filled thoughts at negotiating tables and government centers and in the hearts of world leaders. I pray that each person in the world experiences the peace that passes understanding.

Peace be within your walls, and security within your towers! ... Peace be within you!—Psalm 122:7, 8

One with God, I let nothing disturb the calm peace of my soul.

FEBRUARY 16, 1995

Do I sometimes feel that outer circumstances keep me from experiencing peace of mind? Do I believe that to keep peace in a relationship I have to sacrifice who I am?

True inner peace does not come from a problem-free life or from sacrificing who I am. True inner peace comes from knowing my oneness with God.

I can experience this unshakable kind of peace by becoming still and centering on the presence of God within me. I repeat the affirmation: *God and I are one*, and I begin to feel the peace that comes from knowing I am not alone, that God is always with me.

When I am centered in this peaceful, sacred place within, I can choose to experience peace in every circumstance of my life. In every moment, I choose peace.

Peace I leave with you; my peace I give to you; not as the world gives do I give to you. Let not your hearts be troubled.—John 14:27

All creation is responding to God's message of peace.

DECEMBER 31, 1999

God, I hear Your voice of peace throughout Your diverse and magnificent creation. It is the echo of peace that resounds as the wind gently sways pine trees, as waves rush onto shore, as conversations sparkle with hope. I hear a message of peace being sounded in the world.

God, I pray that all of us here on earth not only hear Your message of peace but also let the love and understanding needed for peace be constantly in our minds and hearts.

Poised on the threshold of a new century, we are ready to enter into a time of love and peace. We see one another as brothers and sisters in the family of God. The spirit of God encourages our love and reverence for each other and for all life.

Put things in order, listen to my appeal, agree with one another, live in peace; and the God of love and peace will be with you.—2 Corinthians 13:11

From the Readers of Daily Word

I've been subscribing to Daily Word *since January 1975. I consider it one of the greatest treasures of my life and feel so blessed to have discovered it.*

—V.F., VENTURA, CALIFORNIA

It brings me so much joy reading my Daily Word. *I start my day with love in my heart and waiting to see what the next day's reading will be. The words of others are so rewarding.*

—J.S., SANTA FE, NEW MEXICO

OMG!! I don't know where to start! Daily Word *seems to know what's going on in my life! The words are perfect each day! I just love it! Thank you so much!*

—R.B., ERSKINE, MINNESOTA

I share the peace within me with those around me as a blessing from my soul.

FEBRUARY 9, 2001

I may find it easy to experience inner peace in the sanctuary of a church or in a favorite meditation garden. Yet I can experience that same peace in the snarl of a traffic jam; a room full of tired, cranky children; or a tension-filled business meeting. I can, because I choose to recognize experiences like these as opportunities to share what blesses, instead of what stresses!

When I am in the midst of a stressful situation, I remember that I serve a greater purpose. With an awareness of God's peace within, I can and I do express an inner calm in all situations. And as I do, I release a surge of peace that encircles me and cushions me so that I don't absorb any outer tension.

Every day is an opportunity to be blessed with peace and to share that blessing.

Those of steadfast mind you keep in peace—in peace because they trust in you.—Isaiah 26:3

Peace fills my soul as I center myself in the love of God.

JUNE 25, 2006

The peace that comes from knowing the love of God is not passive. It is a powerful force for good.

We center ourselves in the love of God, the peace of God. We can bring peace where there seems to be discord in our world—as Jesus did when He spoke the words, "Peace! Be still!" to a stormy sea.

Peace radiates forth from within us, from our very souls as we hold to the truth that God is always with us and we are enfolded in God's love.

Let every breath we breathe and every word we speak express God's peace. As peace flourishes in our hearts and minds, all whom we touch will feel the power of this gift from God through us.

How precious is your steadfast love, O God! All people may take refuge in the shadow of your wings.—Psalm 36:7

I am a center of peace.

NOVEMBER 6, 2014

When I think of inner peace, I picture the eye of a hurricane. Even with the swirling chaos and turmoil, its center is calm and undisturbed. As I turn to the peaceful presence of God within me, I experience tranquility regardless of outer circumstances.

Inner peace comes from faith, intention, and focus. I have faith in God as my source of inner peace. I set my intention to experience serenity in my relationships and interactions. My thoughts and attitudes are focused on peace. With this practice, I experience inner stillness, a calm deep within where nothing can disturb me. I am in the "eye" of the storm. I am the peace that stands secure and strong in the awareness of God.

The priest replied, "Go in peace. The mission you are on is under the eye of the Lord."—Judges 18:6

I see peace in every heart and in every situation.

JULY 13, 2015

My heart joins with others who desire peace in the world. In crowded cities and remote farms, in humid heat and crisp cold, with one voice or with a congregation, we all affirm peace.

As I take a gentle breath, I experience Oneness with all. I center my attention in my heart and connect with others praying at this very moment. I utter the word *peace*, and imagine it echoing in hundreds of languages, dialects, and accents. The power of prayer knows no boundaries and for that I give thanks.

I feel the energy of peace in many hearts around the globe. I affirm: *Peace is possible in every heart and in every situation!* Peace prevails as we breathe as one.

Agree with one another, live in peace; and the God of love and peace will be with you.—2 Corinthians 13:11

My prayers join with others to create world peace.

FEBRUARY 28, 2022

As much as most of us would love to see world peace occur overnight, lasting peace is truly achieved as more and more individuals awaken one by one and contribute their prayerful intention to humanity.

Each praying soul creates an energy that will inevitably find its expression. Just as the individual leaves of an elm tree can contribute to a magnificent cover of shade, so can every peaceful prayer help bring about world peace.

A small act of kindness, forgiving thought, and prayerful hope move us closer to the realization of world peace. The souls who shine their individual lights draw us closer to the moment when the human family sets the world aglow in a light-filled expression of love and peace.

I have said this to you, so that in me you may have peace.
In the world you face persecution. But take courage;
I have conquered the world!—John 16:33

Messages of
FORGIVENESS

Messages of FORGIVENESS

For many, forgiveness is the most challenging spiritual work we are called to practice. *Daily Word* has understood this for 100 years and, time and again, its messages have offered spiritual support to those striving to let go of pain, resentment, and anger about past events. Forgiveness sets us free and allows us to move forward in lightness and peace.

What Can I Do for You?

By Martha Smock

MARCH 1978

What can I do for you? I found myself asking myself this question when it seemed that all my efforts to help someone who had turned to me seemed unavailing. I wondered if I actually was of any help to this person.

At first it seemed so easy, so simple. All this friend needed, I thought, was the right idea, all she needed was to be reminded of the Truth, to be told that God loves her, that God is in charge. I knew I could help her by having faith in her and reassuring her of my faith and prayers.

But time after time I listened as she poured out her feelings of unhappiness, of despair, of self-rejection, of bitterness over the past, of fear of what was ahead.

She always told me how she was trying to pray, to make affirmations of Truth, and she was trying, I knew. But I began to wonder about my part.

I realized that sometimes when we try to help another person, we end up making that person dependent on us. He does not necessarily get help from us, but he gets satisfaction from having someone listen to him without criticism, someone on whom to unload his pent-up feelings of fear, anxiety, unhappiness, frustration.

I realized, too, that there is always the possibility that we, in our own way, become dependent upon the person who turns to us again and again for help. We may unconsciously assume a parental role and feel responsible for him; we may even feel that he cannot get along without us.

I am sure that most persons have had someone in their experience whom they started out trying to help, only to come to the place where they realized that the other person really did not want their help, certainly did not want their advice. What was wanted was someone to be a listening post,

283

someone to lend a sympathetic ear. There was a need to be cheered and bolstered, temporarily.

How do we help another? What can we do for another? Is a listening ear enough? Is sympathy enough? Of some help perhaps, but apparently not enough …

What can *I do for you?*

What I can do for you is something beyond just listening to you, helpful as that may be from time to time. What I can do for you is to pray for you in the highest way that I know, that is, to behold the Christ in you. When I behold the Christ in you, I am beholding that which is innately good and wonderful in you. On a personal level I may see all kinds of things that need changing in you—in your way of thinking, in the way you relate to other persons, in the way you meet life. When I behold the Christ in you, I see nothing to change. I see the changeless Spirit. When I behold the Christ in you, I am never discouraged with you. How can I be discouraged with the Christ? When I behold the Christ in you I do not hear negation, I see the perfect One in you which is always seeking expression. When I behold the Christ in you, I know that you do not need my help or advice, for I know that you have that in you which is your own sure light and guide. I help you most by remembering this and by truly holding to my vision of the Christ in you.

It is easier just to dismiss another person as difficult, as negative, as self-centered than it is to behold the Christ in him. But it is a freeing experience to hold to this prayer of prayers for another person: *I behold the Christ in you.* This is truly to love another person. This is the way I believe Jesus helped those who turned to him. And he said, "By this all men will know that you are my disciples, if you have love for one another."

Perhaps those we are trying to help the most, the ones we are most concerned about, only need our love!

What can I do for you? I can love you with the Christ love. I can love you with a love that accepts you as you are, that loves you for what you are, for when I behold the Christ in you I have every reason to love you.

What can I do for you? I can behold the Christ in you. I can set you free from any bondage on my part, from any attempt on my part to change you. I can let God do His work in you.

What can I do for you? I can love you as God loves you. This is the greatest help I can offer you, this is my most effective prayer for you.

[Martha Smock was editor of *Daily Word* for 33 years—one-third of its first century—from 1944 to 1957 and then from 1964 to 1984.]

I Behold the Christ in You

Frank B. Whitney

I behold the Christ in you,
Here the life of God I see;
I can see a great peace, too,
I can see you whole and free.

I behold the Christ in you,
I can see this as you walk;
I see this in all you do,
I can see this as you talk.

I behold God's love expressed,
I can see you filled with power;
I can see you ever blessed,
See Christ in you, hour by hour.

I behold the Christ in you,
I can see that perfect One;
Led by God in all you do,
I can see God's work is done.

This poem by the creator of Daily Word
*was first published in 1924 and repeated
many times thereafter.*

The forgiving and understanding love of Jesus Christ is expressed through me toward all people.

MARCH 8, 1925

To forgive is to give for—to give some actual, definite good in return for evil given.
—*Lessons in Truth* [H. Emilie Cady]

Jesus' answer to his crucifiers was forgiveness. He understood their thought and forgave them. When he was mocked and reviled, he reviled not. He placed himself in the hands of the Father.

If for wrong you can give good, if for hate you can return love, you understand how to forgive. The secret of forgiveness is the impersonal attitude. If you think of your own personality as being injured and of some person as doing you an injury, you bind yourself to personal consciousness.

To be impersonal in forgiveness is to forgive regardless of the personal situation. This disposition will make you love the one who shows that he has not love. It will make you help that one who would not help you. You will be so filled with a desire to serve the one who is blinded by hate, that you will not be able to hate him.

Keep your vision high. Know that no man has power to harm you. Should he be blinded by the thought that he can do so, it is your duty to let your light shine and help to illuminate his vision. He needs your help, not your censure.

"Father, forgive them; for they know not what they do."

The forgiving power of Christ within me erases from my mind every memory of the misdeeds or shortcomings of myself or others.

DECEMBER 31, 1929

What an effective word for a good mental house cleaning! What a day for getting rid of old memories of misdeeds, shortcomings, and the myriad beliefs that might hold us in bondage to the past! The forgiving power of Christ within us clears from our thought every belief in limitation and shortcoming. Measuring up to the high standard of Christly perfection, we lose sight of the fact that we have ever conceived of ourselves or of others as "missing the mark."

Knowing the truth of the eternal now we give up allegiance to the belief that the past can claim us as its own. We prepare ourselves to enter into a new world, a new day, a new life. We get ready to enter into the mental freedom that comes from relieving the mind of false beliefs. We prepare ourselves to enjoy perfect freedom, freedom based upon the understanding that we are free from every self-imposed belief in adversity. We are forgiven, and, purified and renewed, we enter into the presence of God.

Forgive us our sins; for we ourselves also forgive every one that is indebted to us.—Luke 11:4

The forgiving power of Christ in me now urges me to forgive all who have appeared to harm me, and I forgive thoroughly.

JULY 15, 1934

If you have difficulty in forgiving another who appears to have harmed you, give the matter into God's keeping. Cease trying to reason things out in an intellectual way. You cannot forgive another by reviewing over and over the unhappy incidents of some misunderstanding. You must rise out of such a state of consciousness into a realization of the forgiving power of Christ.

Let the Christ within you recognize and salute the Christ in the one whom you would forgive. Let Christ prompt you to forgive; be willing to respond to His urging. Let Christ within you have His way. The power of His forgiveness must be expressed in you if you would forgive another.

Do you see that forgiveness is not a personal matter, that it does not come from personal consciousness? Forgiveness emanates from the Christ within us. When we forgive, we lose sight of ourselves and let the Christ within us have His way.

Bless Jehovah, O my soul ... Who forgiveth all thine iniquities.—Psalm 103:1, 3

Christ in me is ever prompt to forgive.

JANUARY 23, 1938

Forgiving takes place when we let the Spirit of Christ within us do His perfect work. We cease to think of that which has given us hurt feelings, we rise out of personal consciousness, we give ourselves and our affairs into His keeping.

A person experiences difficulty in forgiving when he gives attention to himself and his personal relations to the exclusion of Christ. He forgives easily when he gives his attention to Christ and His forgiving power to the exclusion of all thought about himself. Do you see that when you withhold forgiveness you do so in order to think about yourself? When you forgive, you think only of the forgiveness of Christ.

You use the power of Christ to forgive when you let Christ work in you. Do you not see what a privilege you exercise when you forgive? When you refuse to forgive, you but refuse to be a channel for the working of Christ.

Be ye kind one to another, tenderhearted, forgiving each other, even as God also in Christ forgave you.—Ephesians 4:32

Father, we rejoice in thy assurance that
we are forgiven as we forgive.

SEPTEMBER 19, 1942

Forgiveness involves a "giving for," a literal return of good for evil. If we try to return evil for evil, we increase strife and contention; but if we literally give good for evil, we render the evil powerless and utterly erase it from our experience.

In the part of the Lord's Prayer that is translated "Forgive us our debts, as we also have forgiven our debtors," an investigation of the original Greek text discloses that true forgiveness involves much more than the release of others from obligations that we may feel they owe us. Forgiveness is but another name for the law of compensation, the law of cause and effect. As we forgive we are forgiven; as we set others free we are set free; as we love others we are loved in return. We put the law into operation by a positive act on our part, and we are rewarded above our expectations.

Let all bitterness, and wrath, and anger, and clamor, and railing, be put away from you, with all malice: and be ye kind one to another, tenderhearted, forgiving each other, even as God also in Christ forgave you.—Ephesians 4:31, 32

Christ in me understands the good intentions of every heart, and I can forgive freely.

AUGUST 11, 1945

We gain nothing by holding onto memories of past hurts and injustices, even if they occurred but a few moments ago. We lose out on much joy by giving even a part of ourselves to the feelings and emotions aroused in us by memories of this sort. When we have come through an experience, we have gained something in wisdom and understanding. This is what we should take for ourselves and let the rest go.

Every person's heart is seeking happiness, but in the seeking he often does and says things that are not true of the intentions of his heart. That is why, if we are to live happily with ourselves and with other persons, we must look deeper than thoughts and actions and understand the good intentions of the heart. When we learn to do this, it is easy for us to forgive ourselves for anything in the past that may not measure up to our present standards, and it becomes easy for us to forgive others who seem not to have measured up to what we expected of them.

For thou, Lord, art ... ready to forgive.—Psalm 86:5

From the Readers of Daily Word

I bring my copy of Daily Word *when I travel. It's amazing how easy it makes sharing God's love!*

—E.E., FARGO, NORTH DAKOTA

It's better than a vitamin! A daily must have! Puts a smile on my face and often having read for the day, all is well again, feeling grateful and restored. My best friend!

—R.T., BOCA RATON, FLORIDA

I look forward each morning to reading the words to get my day started with a positive attitude.

—G.A., MEMPHIS, TENNESSEE

The spirit of love abides within me, and I freely express it as loving-kindness and forgiveness.

NOVEMBER 11, 1950

We are able to express loving-kindness and forgiveness toward all as we open our mind and heart to the forgiving love of Christ and release all unloving thoughts. Through the forgiving love of Christ, we are set free from the belief that we can be mistreated by another or that another can hurt us or cause us unhappiness. The Christ love expressed through us enables us to look beyond all appearances, to keep centered and poised in our own heart and mind, to be understanding and forgiving.

Any tendency to be over-sensitive, to be resentful, or intolerant can be overcome through opening our heart to divine love. When we realize that the very spirit of divine love abides in our heart we realize that our only need is to let it find expression through us. The Christ love blesses; the Christ love forgives; the Christ love understands; the Christ love gives us peace of heart and mind.

I will put my law in their inward parts, and in their heart will I write it.—Jeremiah 31:33

I am forgiving.

NOVEMBER 2, 1956

I am forgiving. I now release all feelings of bitterness, resentment, misunderstanding, injured pride, condemnation, and unforgiveness. I now forgive completely, permanently, lovingly, freely, easily. I now forget all the happenings, all the words, all the acts that seemed to be unpleasant, unhappy, or unkind. I now forgive as God forgives.

I am forgiving. I make forgiveness part of my every prayer, every thought, every word, every act. I give kindness for unkindness; gentleness for rudeness; joy for sorrow; strength for weakness; success for failure; inspiration for despair; enthusiasm for inertia; healing for disease; purpose for uncertainty; courage for fear; faith for doubt; light for darkness.

Even as I forgive others I also forgive myself. I accept and understand the forgiving love of God that is in us all.

I am forgiving and loving toward all persons and all situations.

Give us day by day our daily bread. And forgive us our sins; for we ourselves also forgive every one that is indebted to us.—Luke 11:3, 4

I express God's forgiving love and I am a blessing.

FEBRUARY 19, 1961

It is important that we practice forgiving if we are to be completely happy. Thoughts of ill will and blame do more harm than good. Charles Fillmore has shown us the importance of forgiveness in his pamphlet, "A Sure Remedy." He tells us that forgiveness is a cure for every ill that flesh is heir to. He further tells us to "sit for half an hour every night and mentally forgive everyone against whom you have any ill will or antipathy." It is surprising how well and how quickly this treatment works.

True forgiveness not only releases any sense of blame that we may hold for another person, but it also helps us to forget the incident that needs forgiving and helps us to erase it entirely from our mind. Even though we may have to practice to be forgiving, we can learn to forgive with God's help. And each time we forgive another person, let us remember to send that person a blessing of love. In this way not only will he be blessed, but we will be blessed as well.

Forgive us our sins; for we ourselves also forgive every one.—Luke 11:4

> *I stand firm in the faith that the forgiving love of Jesus Christ sets me free.*

APRIL 25, 1967

There are many instances in the Bible where we are told of Jesus' forgiving love. In some of these instances we wonder how He could have had the greatness of heart to forgive. But forgive He did! Knowing His faith in the ability of all mankind to measure up to His high standard, we are inspired to practice this same forgiving love.

Let us start by forgiving ourselves. Let us forgive petty thoughts, unworthy reactions, self-condemnation, condemnation of others. Let us accept forgiveness for ourselves.

Next let us forgive others. Let us forgive any slights, any sins of omission or commission, any critical or unpleasant word, any thoughtless act, any biased stand. Let us give our love in a forgiving spirit.

Even as we pray to be forgiven and to forgive, we pray to continue to grow in love; for when we love enough there will be nothing to forgive.

Forgive us our debts, as we also have forgiven our debtors.—Matthew 6:12

Forgive! Forget!

[Uncredited]

That slight misdeed of yesterday,
why should it mar today?
The thing he said, the thing you did,
have long since passed away;
For yesterday was but a trial;
today you will succeed,
And from mistakes of yesterday will come
some noble deed.

Forgive yourself for thoughtlessness;
do not condemn the past,
For it is gone with its mistakes;
their memory cannot last;

Forget the failures and misdeeds,
from such experience rise;
Why should you let your head be bowed?
Lift up your heart and eyes.

You'll always have a Friend at hand,
One who'll forgive, forget,
Who sees you not as one who erred,
but's loyal to you yet,
Beholds in you no evil thought or even
trace of sin;
In you He sees the one He loves,
the one who's bound to win.

I am forgiving in all that I say and do.

JANUARY 3, 1973

The forgiving love of God is with us at all times. Knowing this, we can be forgiving in all that we say and do. As His children we have His Spirit of love and forgiveness within us.

If we feel that someone has said or done something hurtful or unloving, let us take a moment right now to forgive this person. Let us enfold him in the forgiving love of God; let us see him as God's child, filled with God's Spirit. Let us release any feeling of criticism or condemnation toward him.

As we go forward, living and radiating the truth to all whose lives we touch, we cannot attract anything that is unkind or unloving to ourselves. Through our awareness of God's forgiving power at work in and through us, we can bless all with whom we live and work and associate. Let us hold fast to the thought that we are forgiving and that we are forgiven, because we are God's children, expressing His Spirit of love, understanding, and forgiveness.

Forbearing one another and, if one has a complaint against another, forgiving each other; as the Lord has forgiven you, so you also must forgive.—Colossians 3:13

Forgiving one another, let us walk in love.

SEPTEMBER 14, 1977

Many letters and calls come to Silent Unity from persons who feel that they cannot forgive themselves for something they did or failed to do. Other letters and calls come from persons who feel that they cannot forgive some other person.

It is true that love, in the highest sense, cannot forgive, for love in the highest sense cannot condemn. Love loves! God, being love, creates us in His image and likeness. We, too, then are love. Where love is, condemnation cannot survive. Placing our need for forgiveness of ourselves or others in God's love, we can be free, we can be kind, understanding, forgiving. However, we must release thoughts of past hurts and mistakes completely to God's love, never reaching in thought and memory to relive them.

When we catch the full impact of the idea that forgiving one another we can walk in love, we have taken the first step toward forgiving ourselves and others.

Be imitators of God, as beloved children.
And walk in love.—Ephesians 5:1-2

Forgiving and forgiven, I begin again on a higher, better level of consciousness.

FEBRUARY 24, 1983

Forgiveness keeps the flow of love unbroken between us and God.

Forgiveness keeps the bond of love intact between us and other people.

Forgiveness cleanses, purifies, and heals our hearts.

Forgiveness brings freedom from unrest.

Forgiveness sets our minds at peace.

Forgiveness soothes our emotions, quiets inner turmoil.

Forgiveness releases the highest and best in us.

Forgiveness sets us free from condemnation of self or others.

Forgiveness wipes the slate clean.

Forgiving and forgiven, we begin again on a higher, better level of consciousness. Our soul rejoices that we are truly learning to love as Jesus Christ taught us to love, to forgive as Jesus Christ taught us to forgive.

Condemn not, and you will not be condemned; forgive, and you will be forgiven.—Luke 6:37

I speak the word of forgiveness to
myself and to others.

JULY 12, 1986

There is a word that replaces conflict with understanding and anxiety with peace of mind. This word is *forgive*. If I have spoken out of turn or have done something I instantly regretted, I speak the word of forgiveness to myself. I look past my actions to the love of God in my heart. This love enables me to reach out to others and say, "Forgive me."

If someone has been thoughtless or unkind, I speak the word of forgiveness and seek to heal any division. I look past the action to the love of God indwelling every heart. This love enables me to say to others, "I forgive you."

Forgiveness is a mighty word and one that I feel comfortable speaking. The practice and expression of forgiveness brings such joy and harmony that I delight in speaking it again and again. In forgiveness, the stumbling blocks to understanding and happiness have been removed.

Be kind to one another, tenderhearted, forgiving one
another, as God in Christ forgave you.—Ephesians 4:32

I am willing to forgive, and I do forgive.

JANUARY 11, 1992

One of the ways in which we experience divine love is through forgiveness. True and lasting peace of mind and well-being are maintained when we are forgiving. The blessing of forgiveness heals any sense of separation between us and others.

Even though we feel that we cannot forgive, we can. We do not prolong our pain by continuing to focus on unforgiveness. In becoming willing to forgive, we free ourselves from the bondage of an unforgiving attitude and allow divine love to flow through us unhindered.

Energy that once was used to maintain an unmoving stance is transformed into productive, constructive, loving energy. Energy is made manifest as health on every level, abundance in all our affairs, and wisdom in all our relationships.

Put on then, as God's chosen ones, holy and beloved, compassion, kindness, lowliness, meekness, and patience, forgiving each other.—Colossians 3:12-13

I forgive and experience the
exhilaration of forgiveness.

JUNE 6, 1996

Have you ever wondered why it's so important to forgive? Sure, we all feel better when someone forgives us for something we've done, but what's in it for us if we are doing the forgiving?

We forgive because we must—not because it's something we've been told to do or forced to do, but because it's the only way to gain true freedom—freedom from the past and freedom to live fully now.

So we forgive. As we bring to mind any people we want to forgive—because of major hurts and minor inconveniences—let's make sure we also include ourselves. It doesn't do any good to forgive others if we continue to hold a grudge against ourselves.

Isn't it exhilarating—this wonderful sense of freedom that is filling our minds and hearts? We are reaping the benefits of our loving actions!

Whenever you stand praying, forgive.—Mark 11:25

From the Readers of Daily Word

I start my day every day with my Daily Word *after my daily prayer to God every morning. I just love my* Daily Word *so much.*

—R.R., TROY, NEW YORK

I really enjoy reading Daily Word—*it just makes my day. I have been going through a lot and just reading* Daily Word *helps me to get through each day.*

—M.A., FLETCHER, NORTH CAROLINA

I read it every day! It means the world to me! I love it!

—B.L., DADE CITY, FLORIDA

The love of God enables me to release the past and forgive myself.

JUNE 13, 2003

Why is it sometimes easier for me to forgive others than it is for me to forgive myself? Rather than carry a burden of guilt with me wherever I go, I am learning to release the past and forgive myself by turning everything over to God in prayer.

Thank You, God, for helping me understand that by forgiving myself I am recognizing that whatever happened was an opportunity for me to learn from a mistake. And I am grateful that I will not have to repeat it.

Dear God, I know that through Your loving spirit within me, I have the strength to release the past and forgive myself fully and completely.

Do not remember the former things, or consider the things of old. I am about to do a new thing; now it springs forth, do you not perceive it?—Isaiah 43:18-19

*I open my heart to God and receive
the blessing that forgiveness brings me.*

MARCH 13, 2006

Jesus taught His followers the importance of giving and receiving forgiveness with a parable: A master had mercy on a servant and forgave him the debt he owed. This same servant refused to forgive another servant's debt. When the master found out, he had the unforgiving servant's debt restored.

Forgiveness is a natural function of the principle of giving and receiving. As I release the past, I open my heart to God, the forgiving Spirit within me and everyone.

My forgiveness of myself is related to my forgiveness of others, because my willingness to forgive others inspires me to also forgive myself. My life is enriched as this cycle of giving and receiving continues to bless me and all my relationships.

---

*Create in me a clean heart, O God, and put a new
and right spirit within me.—Psalm 51:10*

When I forgive, I release the past and embody the present.

AUGUST 11, 2012

A closed heart cannot receive love and joy. A clenched fist cannot accept an outstretched hand. Today I give myself the gift of forgiveness, as I open my heart—myself—to living in love.

I can cling to hurtful experiences from the past or surrender them for a better life now. As I release attachment to a painful memory, I allow myself to replace pain with peace, hurt with joy.

Forgiving does not mean condoning hurtful actions. Forgiveness means releasing the pain and reclaiming my life. When I forgive, I am freed to move beyond the unchangeable past into a new experience of divine possibilities.

Bear with one another and, if anyone has a complaint against another, forgive each other; just as the Lord has forgiven you.—Colossians 3:13

As I forgive myself, I can forgive others.

JANUARY 24, 2019

The words I say and choices I make can sometimes hurt others, and I may feel regret for something I've said or done. Forgiving others is one of the keys to living free. Before I can truly forgive anyone else, however, I must first be willing to forgive myself. At my core, I am divine. On the outside, I am a human being who can make mistakes and fall short of my best.

I take time to reflect on what happened and then pause, inhaling a deep, cleansing breath. Moving from human judgment into the space of divine love, I embrace the lesson available to me. This is a moment of discovery—an opportunity to find compassion for myself and others. I make amends, knowing that at the core of forgiveness is mercy, love, and grace.

Blessed are the merciful, for they will receive mercy.
—Matthew 5:7

Forgiveness heals my heart.

FEBRUARY 24, 2022

Few things have the constricting effect on my heart that resentment does. Even if I believe my anger is justified, I realize I am paying too high a price by holding on to it and letting it fester. Withholding forgiveness is a punishment I inflict only upon myself. Nothing is worth sacrificing my peace of mind.

Today I shift my thoughts away from what someone said or did that caused me to feel hurt. Instead, I place my attention on healing through forgiveness. I bless my tenderest self with thoughts of love and peace. Even if this is difficult at first, I keep at it, trusting that divine love within will soften my heart.

I begin to open myself to forgiveness. This burgeoning willingness is the first small step toward healing my heart.

For you, O Lord, are good and forgiving, abounding in steadfast love to all who call on you.—Psalm 86:5

Chapter 12

Messages of
GRACE

Messages of GRACE

Interestingly, *grace* was not a word used often in the first few decades of *Daily Word*'s publication. It was mentioned in some messages but not chosen as a frequent topic until at least the 1940s. Still, *Daily Word* has always made it clear that the more we align ourselves with God consciousness, the more we experience and appreciate the many blessings of our lives. Our needs are fulfilled, and our path is clear.

Strength, Service, and the Power of the Word

By Meg McConahey

SEPTEMBER/OCTOBER 2020

When an onslaught of mammoth rains and mudslides engulfed northern Argentina three years ago, Beatriz and Frank Bell knew the local people would need more than emergency food, clothing, and housing to help them recover.

In the wake of the catastrophe, the couple made their way into some of the poorest and hardest hit communities, delivering messages of hope, faith, and healing.

The Bells came bearing copies of *Mensajes de Esperanza de La Palabra Diaria* (*Messages of Hope from Daily Word*). As they walked through the village, sometimes door-to-door, open hands eagerly reached for the magazine, filled with spiritual reminders that the power of God's healing love is present, even in the most challenging times.

Their first destination? Volcán, a tiny, Andean village 600 miles from their home, where landslides in January 2017 killed four people and displaced 1,000. Roads were impassable and buildings stuck like islands in the mud. Most of the homes in the town of 1,700 were inundated with up to 31 inches of muck.

Spreading the Ministry of Daily Word *Internationally*

For 12 years this has been the boots-on-the-ground ministry for the Bells: ensuring that *Daily Word* (in Spanish, *La Palabra Diaria*) is available in a country where the postal service is unreliable and persistent recession and economic crises have made it hard for people to afford an international subscription.

Their mission also took them that spring to La Madrid, a town of 2,800 in the flood-prone province of Tucumán, where overflowing waters forced

> "Something that I learned at that time that started a shift in my perception of life," she said, "was that there were not two powers fighting in the universe, as I believed, but there was one presence and one power, God, and it was absolute good."—Beatriz Bell

most of the community to evacuate, some permanently. The determined couple entered via a temporary bypass; the only highway into the village was cut to allow the town to drain.

By the time they arrived in May in their Ford pickup filled with magazines, both communities were recovering physically. But many people still grappled with the lingering psychological and emotional trauma and were hungry for the hope that comes with spiritual affirmation.

The Bells visited health centers, a tribal arts and crafts center, and a municipal relief center. They left magazines with community leaders to distribute and gave magazines to the hospital patients.

"We found that people were very grateful for this support," Beatriz said. "When we have brought issues to the hospital in our area and

explained about the spiritual and positive content, they said it was very comforting for them in those difficult times."

The Bells had anticipated this need well before the heavy rains. With weather-related disasters becoming increasingly common in Argentina, they arranged in 2016 to print a Spanish-language special edition of *Messages of Hope from Daily Word*.

"We keep going knowing that God is our Source."

The Creative Spark for a New Calling

Unlike the *Daily Word* periodical, its entries were undated. Underwritten with help from donations, it was free, as the Bells put it, "delivered to people in Argentina who are experiencing difficult situations, so they will have something of inspiration and hope."

Beatriz knew from experience the uplifting power of those daily messages of hope, courage, and abundance. She discovered *La Palabra Diaria* in 1995 when she joined a metaphysics study group in her hometown of Córdoba. She felt excited by Unity and *Daily Word*, which teach that we cocreate our reality with God through our thoughts and prayers.

"Something that I learned at that time that started a shift in my perception of life," she said, "was that there were not two powers fighting in the universe, as I believed, but there was one presence and one power, God, and it was absolute good.

"The other revelation to me was that a spark of this presence and power was in me. The next awakening ideas were about the creative power of thought and the power of prayer."

Beatriz, who had a long career as an attorney and judge, found through prayer a new calling in the ministry, a means of sharing with others the comfort and the abundance of blessings that are ever present when our hearts and eyes are open to see them.

While enrolled in the International Students Program at Unity Village in Missouri, Beatriz met her future husband, Frank, and together they established Unity, Sembrando Luz (Unity, Sowing Light), an alternative ministry that provided personal and spiritual support to Spanish speakers in their Olathe, Kansas, community.

The Challenges of Bringing La Palabra Diaria to Argentina

When Frank, a technician with the U.S. Federal Aviation Administration, retired in 2008, they moved their outreach ministry to South America. From their home in Villa La Bolsa, a scenic town in north central Argentina, they embarked on a mission of distributing *Daily Word*, a magazine with a circulation of 400,000 copies in 19 countries, but almost no presence in Argentina.

They now sell approximately 220 copies of each issue, doing everything they can to keep the price affordable during the country's financial crisis. Their distribution efforts now extend to in-person sales through Unity centers and study groups in several provinces as well as to a growing digital and radio ministry.

When we take on new callings, the efforts are not always smooth, and require persistence and faith as we keep our minds open to new pathways around obstacles.

"Even as we have faced challenges, we always attempt to be grounded in our spiritual principles. As we do that, we can realize that our inner guidance never makes a mistake. The more we trust, the more we see."

The Bells met some resistance when they tried to find a printer.

"The printer representative tried to discourage us, saying it will cost us more to print the magazine in Argentina than to have it imported. We left depressed," Beatriz recalled. "We prayed for guidance and calmly continued looking for other printers."

They finally found a printer who would work with them, and continues to do so, more than a decade later. Printing costs remain a challenge.

"However, we keep going knowing that God is our Source. We have never changed the quality of the paper or printing but have cut costs by reducing the number of issues printed to more accurately reflect the demand," Beatriz said.

A Community for La Palabra Diaria *Messages Online and on the Air*

They have fostered community by establishing a new Unity study group in Buenos Aires and use social media to share *Daily Word* with a wider audience at little to no cost. For several years the Bells have maintained an abbreviated Facebook page, *La Palabra Diaria en Argentina*, in which they share daily affirmations and quotes. They currently have 854 followers.

This past year, after being interviewed by the online radio program *La Magia del Silencio* about *Daily Word* and its messages of spiritual assurance, they were invited to do a weekly program covering spiritual topics such as forgiveness, the power of thought, gratitude, and inner guidance. Through their efforts, Frank and Beatriz Bell have found renewed meaning in work that feeds their spirits but also is in service to others.

"At this moment we can say that we feel really blessed and grateful," Beatriz said. "Even as we have faced challenges, we always attempt to be grounded in our spiritual principles. As we do that, we can realize that our inner guidance never makes a mistake. The more we trust, the more we see."

Meg McConahey is a daily newspaper reporter in Northern California and former board president of Unity of Santa Rosa, California.

My Soul Has Walked with Holy Things

Priscilla Drennen

My soul has walked with lovely things today:
Pine trees that rose in simple majesty!
Cool shadows curtained all the mossy way;
The path seemed one of sacred mystery.
White-crested waves upon the golden sand,
The flight of graceful seagulls winging near,
The feel of pussy willows in my hand,
The song of whispering winds upon my ear.
The earth wash'd clean by spring's warm
    slanting rain,
All new and fresh as morning's rosy glow.
Reverberations of an old refrain,
Melodic notes that fell so sweet and low.

My soul has walked with precious things
    today:
Deep joy reflected in a loved one's eyes;
And faith that teaches better how to pray
Nor doubts the power that in Spirit lies.
A moment of uncertainty was changed
My God's assurance of His presence near:
His power and wisdom have my life arranged,
His love is over all that I hold dear,
His peace is now my own to have and share,
His friendly touch a sense of oneness brings:
I have the clear conviction of his care—
Ah, yes, my soul has walked with holy things.

No adverse experience can injure me in any way. I am eternally established in the goodness and the truth of God.

APRIL 16, 1926

Experiences should help us to higher ground. Those that are adverse should be as beneficial, in this way, as those that we consider pleasant and helpful. However, regardless of the experience, one should not feel that it gives him permanent injury.

There are those who feel that some experience has put an eternal blight upon their souls. They need to know that change of thought will redeem them.

In some churches confession is used with a view to purging the consciousness of past sins and of establishing the assurance of forgiveness. Confession to God serves to remove the thorn in the flesh, and to replace it with a consciousness of purification. The individual leaves the confessional with the feeling that his adverse experience has been wiped away and that he is restored again to the graces of God.

The growing pond lily, unconcerned by the muddy and murky things about it, pushes upward to the light of the sun. When it opens on the surface of the water there is no sign of its past experiences, its life in the mud. In the countenance of the lily is reflected the light of the sun.

The sun ... passeth through pollutions and itself remains as pure as before.—Francis Bacon

Moment by moment I am growing in the consciousness of my innate perfection.

FEBRUARY 24, 1929

I know that, so long as I grow in spiritual consciousness, just so long shall I continue to develop mentally, physically, and spiritually. With this in mind, I daily develop my spiritual consciousness. I behold the blueprint which I am to follow in living a well-rounded life.

I give up every belief which would tend to make me crystallized or stagnant in mind or in body. I give up every prejudice, every resistance to growth. I erase from my consciousness every belief which would bind me to limitation. Moment by moment I am growing. I am developing into the perfect child of God which I am in Truth. I let the Christ within me express Himself easily and freely.

My body is developing healthily and symmetrically. I develop every cell, nerve, gland, muscle, and bone as it should be developed in a healthy body. I know that the power of Spirit now active within me causes my body to become completely the temple of God, for such it is in Spirit.

Grow in the grace and knowledge of our Lord and Saviour Jesus Christ.—2 Peter 3:18

The blessings of heaven are now showered upon me and I am truly blessed by God.

NOVEMBER 30, 1931

Blessings come to us as heavenly benedictions. They include wisdom, peace, love, health, and plenty. They are God's favors and graces showered upon us. They come as heaven-sent messengers to keep our eyes fixed upon the goodness of God and the bounty of heaven.

The student of practical Christianity, one who recognizes the omnipresence of God and His blessings, usually finds himself well blessed with good things. He knows no absence of good. He does not think of himself as denied any good thing. He knows that he is being continually blessed by God.

If you would have the blessing of health, look to heaven for it. Look away from weakness and disease. Turn your vision heavenward and behold the windows of heaven opening in order to give you its largest blessing—perfect health. The blessing of wisdom but prepares the way for the coming of perfect health—perfect harmony of mind, soul, and body.

If you would be blessed with prosperity and success, look to the Lord for this.

The blessing of Jehovah, it make thee rich.—Proverbs 10:22

I am strong in the grace and power of the Lord.

DECEMBER 3, 1940

The Spirit of the Lord is the Spirit of infinite grace. God's grace found its greatest expression through the mind and heart of Jesus Christ, and it is promised that I too can accomplish the things that He accomplished if I but let the same Spirit express itself through me.

As I go forth this day to perform the work that is my appointed task, I take with me the remembrance that my obligation to others is love. In my zealous desire to accomplish the greater things through Truth I shall not ignore the demands of common courtesy and consideration. I shall be quick to give a word of encouragement where it is needed, to commend another for his sincere efforts, and to applaud the successes of my fellow men. Praise is a gift that everyone can afford, yet its value cannot be measured by worldly standards.

I let my light shine this day in love and grace, and all good things are made possible to me.

That the grace, being multiplied through the many, may cause the thanksgiving to abound unto the glory of God.—2 Corinthians 4:15

> *God's grace is poured out upon me.*
> *I am renewed, vitalized, uplifted.*

SEPTEMBER 28, 1944

One of the heaviest burdens that we human beings put upon ourselves is that of self-condemnation, blaming ourselves for our real or fancied wrongdoings, or for our failures. So long as we permit ourselves to carry this burden, we can make little spiritual progress.

It is right for us to recognize our shortcomings, and to rectify as far as is humanly possible any offenses that we have committed against our fellow man. But once we have done all we can do in this respect, we need to cease our human efforts, forgive ourselves, and in humbleness of heart let God's law of grace engulf our feeling of guilt or blame.

The law of grace may be stated thus: "As ye forgive, ye are forgiven." Only when we forgive ourselves do we open the way for God's grace to be poured out upon us. Then a sense of peace and well-being suffuses us. We know that all is well. We are renewed, vitalized, uplifted, filled with life abundant, exalted.

My servant ... shall be exalted and lifted up,
and shall be very high.—Isaiah 52:13

From the Readers of Daily Word

Very helpful to stay focused on the divine activity in my life.
—M.N., VALPARAISO, INDIANA

My husband and I start each morning with reading our Daily Word *and prayer. We have been married 43 years and the* Daily Word *has been on our table every year.*
—J.J., MARION, OHIO

On so many occasions, to family and friends who have needed words from the heart of "Jesus," sharing with them Daily Word *at the exact moment of their need has been and is so exciting! Thanks to you and Jesus above all else.*
—K.D., OWENSBORO, KENTUCKY

As I keep my mind centered in the presence of God,
His loving spirit does the work.

JANUARY 14, 1950

The Spirit of God in me is the one and only healer, the one and only light that can dispel all darkness from my consciousness, I cannot heal myself by mental effort or will power, so I do not try. Rather I relax and let go, and I place my trust in the Father within, to whom all things are possible.

I do not feel it necessary to tell my needs to God, one by one, for He knows my every need even before I tell Him. Therefore I relax and trust His all-knowing wisdom. I do not believe that I must consciously direct the power of God to this or that specific condition, for I believe that as I quietly rest in His presence within and about me, steadfastly keeping my thoughts on Him, He makes the necessary outer adjustments.

The deeper my silence, the greater my trust in His ability to do the work, the more quickly will the wellsprings of good within me overflow into all departments of my life and make me every whit whole.

For by grace have ye been saved through faith; and that not of yourselves, it is the gift of God.—Ephesians 2:8

God's grace is sufficient.

JULY 13, 1956

Beloved, do you need special strength for today? Does dawn find you dreading the hours ahead?

Be of good cheer. You have nothing to fear. Your affairs are in the hands of almighty God, the heavenly Father who loves and cares for you. You have only to loose your worries to realize that His grace is, indeed, sufficient for you.

If there is a deadline for some task that has seemed beyond your strength and endurance, be still, be very still, and know that God is loving and all-powerful. With His strength to aid you, no task is impossible.

Is this a day when you make a change and you dread the unfamiliar? Lay aside your dread. God is as near in the unknown as in the familiar. Look eagerly for the blessings that He will give in the new situation.

Is this the anniversary of a loss or disappointment? Do not bring back the pain of days that are past. Instead, thank God for His sustaining grace and for His presence with you.

Be of good cheer; I have overcome the world.—John 16:33

> *I no longer condemn myself or others for past mistakes and I am free through the love and grace of God.*

MARCH 30, 1962

There is forgiveness. It is the gift of God. No matter what mistakes I have made in the past, I accept all experiences as a divine call to come up higher.

I accept forgiveness with joy. God's love now flows through me to bless and release me. God's love assures me that I cannot fall from His grace or depart from His care.

God's love flows out from me to others. God's love removes from my mind and heart any resentment, prejudice, or enmity that I may feel toward another person. God's love quickens me with the realization that we are all spiritual children in the process of growing and unfolding. I forgive and set free any persons in my life who have hurt or upset me, and I am forgiven and set free.

I rejoice in the present moment, in the present opportunity to express God's love.

I rejoice, for I am free through the love and grace of God.

By grace have ye been saved through faith; and that not of yourselves, it is the gift of God.—Ephesians 2:8

I accept God's grace in my life.

SEPTEMBER 14, 1969

The grace of God is a climate of progress in which the ideals of spiritual growth are paramount. It is a condition of being in which freedom reigns.

When anyone dares to accept those standards of being which God offers, he graduates from the limited causes of human mistakes into the grace of a freer way of conduct.

Whatever it is that we desire to experience, which will reveal more grace in our life, is ours right now, spiritually. We may claim it by affirmation. It is ours by our decree. Affirmative prayer allows us to take hold of a right idea and make it our own.

Under grace we are able to exercise freedom that elevates us to the higher laws of love, forgiveness, and peace.

Under grace we discover inner dynamics that permit us to prove our best abilities in the face of every human challenge.

Under grace we are free indeed.

Through him we have obtained access to this grace in which we stand, and we rejoice in our hope of sharing the glory of God.—Romans 5:2

October Answer

James Dillet Freeman

Fall is fulfillment, as spring was a hope.
Spring had a vision toward which life could grope;
But on an autumn afternoon we know
The final knowledge of all things that grow.
All that the fond heart hoped is fruited here;
Now in the fall, the yellow of the year
The high tide of content all spring longed for,
Dreamed of, comes true, yet we go dreaming more.
Only October has these perfect days
That wear the heavens like a golden haze
Of beauty, more than heaped-up heart can hold,
Spilling forth showers of leaves like miser's gold,
Fields deep with peace, still music in the air:
October answer to an April prayer!

I open my heart to God's grace.

SEPTEMBER 28, 1972

It has been said: "The wind of God's grace is forever blowing; one has but to unfurl the sails of his heart and catch the ever-flowing breeze."

Grace is a free gift from God. In the stillness of each heart God constantly murmurs, "Know ye not that ye are a son of the Most High?" In our busy life this still small voice is often not heard. We may believe that we just do not have the time to take a few minutes and be still.

This day I do take the necessary time and turn all the energies of my mind within. When my mind becomes still, I unfurl the sails of my heart fully and catch the ever-flowing breeze. Gently, lovingly this awareness wells up within my heart until I feel the full impact of its presence, until my heart becomes full to overflowing. I go forth, knowing beyond a doubt that God's grace is forever guiding me, directing me to a safe harbor away from all the apparent storms of life. I realize that such storms are only on the surface, that in God's grace I am forever secure.

And from his fulness have we all received,
grace upon grace.—John 1:16

I walk in the way of God's grace;
I grow in understanding and love.

DECEMBER 9, 1979

The way of God's grace is a beautiful, peaceful, loving way. It is a way of forgiveness and love, of true understanding and compassion. In our communion with the gentle presence of the Christ within us, we grow in our desire and ability to let feelings of gentleness and peace come forth.

We can live the life of grace with ease as we follow our inner guidance. Whatever we are called upon to understand and forgive becomes a stepping-stone on our path of growth and unfoldment. Each time we make the effort to express forgiveness and understanding, we are stepping into a brighter, happier way of life. The understanding and compassion we give to others becomes our own. Our lives and the lives of those around us are enriched with God's grace and goodness, with forgiveness and peace, and forgiveness and peace shall forever abide with us.

The Lord will grant you understanding in everything.
—2 Timothy 2:7

God has given me a mind of wisdom and a heart of love.

AUGUST 28, 1983

Let us consider how skillfully we are fashioned by our Creator. The Psalmist declares that we are created a little lower than the angels! How magnificent our gifts and abilities truly are. God has given us a mind of wisdom and a heart of love. These are indeed splendid tools for effective living.

With God's gift of wisdom we can focus our thoughts on those things which promote an awareness of His infinite blessings. With our minds guided by God's wisdom we can be channels through which His forgiveness, patience, acceptance, and grace flow into our lives and through us into the lives of others.

With God's gift of love we can approach every situation and all people with peace and understanding. With our hearts centered in love we are able to behold the Christ in all those with whom we share our lives.

For wisdom will come into your heart, and knowledge will be pleasant to your soul.—Proverbs 2:10

Centered and poised in the presence of God, I move through the activities of this day easily and gracefully.

JANUARY 17, 1985

Persons who have learned to live in the conscious awareness of the presence of God have a certain glow about them. They are calm and collected and they radiate a poised, peaceful attitude. Their eyes sparkle with love and reflect the serenity of a peaceful soul. They move unhurriedly, easily, and gracefully through the activities of the day.

Today I choose to live in the conscious awareness of the presence of God. I relax the tense hold I may have held on life and place everything lovingly in the hands of the Father. Through the presence of God within me, I have the strength and power, wisdom and understanding, joy and enthusiasm to move forward in faith to do those things which are mine to do.

Centered and poised in the presence of God, I move through the activities of this day easily and gracefully.

My presence will go with you.—Exodus 33:14

I am healed and made whole through the loving grace of God.

JUNE 26, 1993

God is love, and through God's love for me I have been blessed with the greatest of all gifts—the gift of divine grace.

God's love for me is changeless and eternal; there is nothing I can do that will make God love me less. The activity of grace, however, brings divine love to a more personal level of meaning in my life, for through grace I am healed and made whole.

Like divine love, grace is not something I have to work for or earn. Grace is always mine just as divine love is always mine as a beloved child of God.

I am healed and made whole through the loving grace of God. As I accept God's love and grace into my life, I open the way for greater healing of mind, body, and relationships.

Let us then with confidence draw near to the throne of grace, that we may receive mercy and find grace to help in time of need.—Hebrews 4:16

> *Through grace, I am constantly receiving the love and guidance of God.*

OCTOBER 19, 1999

By the grace of God, I am always more than I think I can be. I can always do more than I believe I can do.

Grace is the love of God that goes before me, making my way a path of peace, encouraging me on toward my goals, and assuring me that I am important and needed in God's world.

I am delighted with the results when I trust in the grace of God to help me through a challenge or to move me forward in an achievement. The joy I experience is a celebration of what God has done through me.

In those times when I seem to fall short of my goal, I realize that I can and will do better by the grace of God. Grace is there to ease my disappointment and to open the way for something that is even better than the goal I had been working toward.

Stephen, full of grace and power, did great wonders and signs among the people.—Acts 6:8

From the Readers of *Daily Word*

It always seems that the reading pertains to something I am going through. It helps to clarify, to think [through] difficulty, and change an attitude and/or give me peace.
                              —S.H., OAK FOREST, ILLINOIS

The Daily Word *starts my day and has for many years. Reminds me that no matter what is happening in my life, God is here with me.*
                              —M.Y., MANAWA, WISCONSIN

I am lost without the lessons each day—seem to suit my every need!
                              —J.R., LADY LAKE, FLORIDA

God's grace is blessing me in unlimited ways.

NOVEMBER 18, 2004

By the very nature of my being as a creation of God, I have been given the gift of God's grace. This gift is the unconditional and everlasting love of God for me. Knowing who I am—a child of God—I am enriched to the very core of my being.

As my growing awareness of God's grace uplifts my thoughts and feelings, a cornucopia of divine inspiration is revealed to me. I am a joy-filled, appreciative recipient of God's grace. I acknowledge the love and guidance that support me and prepare me for every moment of life. I give thanks for my blessings, too numerous to mention, and I move forward with an inner peace that comes from viewing the future with positive expectation. God's grace blesses me, and I pass my blessing along as I share my joy with others.

Grace, mercy, and peace will be with us from God the Father and from Jesus Christ, the Father's Son, in truth and love.—2 John 1:3

God's grace refreshes and renews me.

SEPTEMBER 1, 2009

Without being asked, rain refreshes the parched earth, a mother tends to her child's every need, and the wind gently blows a sailboat across the water.

Without being asked, divine grace pours blessings upon me and reminds me I am God's beloved. Grace provides inspiring thoughts that nudge me in the direction of my highest good.

If I become discouraged, grace encourages me to begin again. Grace leads me to forgive myself and others, thus freeing me from the burden of anger and pain.

Through every day of my life, I am refreshed and renewed by the blessings of God's grace.

Everything is for your sake, so that grace ... may increase thanksgiving, to the glory of God.—2 Corinthians 4:15

I receive the grace of God.

OCTOBER 22, 2013

Grace is the moment the flower blooms, the subtle harmony from a musical instrument, the sweet breeze of autumn, a relaxed breath.

Grace happens when I let go and open the doors of my soul to God's guidance. Grace arrives as effortlessly as the falling leaves when I stop trying to figure out life and just let it be through me. I don't have to do anything to earn grace; it arises when I surrender.

Grace is the touch of God letting me know that, at any time, I can start over. It is the promise of a new beginning guided by Divine Love. No matter what has happened in the past, knowing I am worthy, I open my heart to the luminous light of grace.

Daughter, your faith has made you well; go in peace, and be healed of your disease.—Mark 5:34

I am the activity of God expressing as me.

AUGUST 31, 2018

The grace of God is like a flowing river—a wellspring of light, love, and abundance—that gently leads me through the circumstances of life. I don't need to worry about why or how God's grace is revealed. I trust that through it, I will have the insight, resources, and skills to make good things happen in my life.

"My grace is sufficient for you." These words from the apostle Paul to the Corinthians are a reminder that I have within me the necessities to live a free and abundant life. Whatever my need, whatever I am concerned about, I can be sure that through divine grace, the answer will be sufficient for me and those I care about. God's grace is more than enough for me because *I am the activity of God expressing as me.*

By the grace of God I am what I am.—1 Corinthians 15:10

The grace of God flows freely through me.

JANUARY 31, 2022

Within the turbulence of a storm exists the delicate beauty and perfection of the raindrop. Filled with renewing, cleansing water, each drop contains the nourishing promise of new life.

I can think of grace the same way. No matter the storm, the presence of God is within it, vibrantly alive and discoverable in every detail. When life's hurricanes arrive, infinite grace shelters me from the deluge.

It is easier to weather a downpour if I am prepared and protected, so I step confidently into the powerful shelter of my faith. Mindful of my every blessing, I cherish all the gratitude and grace I can find. I don't simply ride out the storm, I grow through it, appreciating the power and majesty of each precious drop of rain.

From his fullness we have all received, grace upon grace.
—John 1:16

Messages of

PROTECTION
AND
COMFORT

Messages of
PROTECTION
AND COMFORT

With the Unity emphasis on our spiritual nature and the Divine within, it might be hard to conceptualize protection and comfort from God. How does it come from within? This question was answered as early as 1927 in a *Daily Word* entry: "God is never apart or away from man. At the center of man's being, God abides. God is a well-spring of joy to all who find Him. He is a source of joy and comfort." The presence that dwells within us, also called our Christ essence, infuses us with the energy of protection and comfort. We have access to all that God is because we are made in the image and likeness of the Divine.

A New Life, A New Song

By Daniel Nahmod

SEPTEMBER/OCTOBER 2009

A little more than 10 years ago, I experienced an awakening. Day after day, I had sat at my desk at my computer programming job, more or less pretending to work. I realized the life I was living was a life I no longer wanted to live.

I decided to move from Chicago to Los Angeles, and in 1998, I began my new life as a singer/songwriter. Soon after I arrived, I volunteered at Cedars-Sinai Medical Center with my guitar, singing for patients, nurses, and administrators. I sang for people in comas and watched as they moved to the rhythm of the music. Elderly patients would hum along to familiar songs.

I've always enjoyed making music to uplift. I come from a family that suffered terribly in the Holocaust. So it's no accident that the intention of my music is to heal the divisions, hatreds, and fears. I don't claim that a song can change the world. But I've seen how the music and the message can make walls invisible for a few minutes at a time.

In 2005, just after Hurricane Katrina, I received a call from my friend, Rev. Richard Rogers … We talked about how we might be of help to the people of New Orleans and the Gulf Coast.

We met at the Houston airport and drove to the Houston Astrodome, where thousands of displaced people filled this gigantic building. They were people without homes to go to, without a job to report to, without a structure to their lives. Richard walked the floor shaking hands, hugging people, offering comfort. I played my guitar and sang songs during two of the most intense and profoundly heartbreaking days I have ever experienced.

The fear and absolute bewilderment were palpable. As I walked from cot to cot, in the middle of the most chaotic, disruptive, disturbing scene I'd ever witnessed, I stopped frequently to talk with individuals. I came to one elderly woman sitting on her cot, holding her head in her hands. A little girl, her granddaughter, was sitting by her.

I asked this woman, "Would you like to hear a song?" She waved her hands in the air as if to say, "whatever." I sat down next to her and asked, "Would you do me a favor? I think you're going to know this song. Close your eyes and sing it with me."

I started playing "What a Wonderful World," and she began to sing ever so quietly with me. Her eyes were closed and so were her granddaughter's. I closed my eyes as well, and for four minutes or so there was no Astrodome, no despair, no Katrina. There was just the beauty of that song. We were lifted up and transported in—not physically, but emotionally and spiritually—to the safest place imaginable.

In those few moments, the work of my life gained greater clarity. I am aware that when I sing a song, whether it's in a hospital room or a large auditorium, for four or five minutes I am sharing a vision. It's a feeling, an instinct, and hopefully a wisdom. It's a drop of consciousness—a safe space.

As a musician, I don't believe it's my responsibility to change the world or even to change the person in front of me. My responsibility is simply to dig as deep as I can, feel as authentically as I can, and share my consciousness. Singing has become a way I pray. There is a place I go when I'm singing, a place where I feel every word as a vibration or energy or consciousness, a place of real peace and love.

I feel blessed that I can share with others by singing and writing songs. Yet I know if I were only to have sung "What a Wonderful World" with the woman and her granddaughter at the Astrodome, just that song, that would have been enough for a lifetime.

Singer/songwriter Daniel Nahmod shares his message of peace, love, and compassion with audiences around the world. Visit *danielnahmod.com*.

In the Shelter of His Love

Ella Morgan Spafard

In the shelter of God's love you are resting,
Safe on land, on sea, and air.
In His promise keep on trusting;
Never need you have a care.
God has promised you protection.
Perfect faith I now declare:
In God's love you are abiding,
And God is everywhere:
Safe, safe, safe,
In the shelter of God's love.

My consciousness of God as my deliverer rescues me from every adverse situation and I abide in his presence of peace and joy.

DECEMBER 20, 1925

The "bringing it to pass" is the work of ... a Presence ... which will always rush to our rescue when we trust it.—Miscellaneous Writings

When one finds himself in an adverse situation, he may be comforted by knowing that his deliverance is at hand. Since his plight is the result of his adverse consciousness, by his high consciousness of truth will come his deliverance.

What has seemed an evil obsession will be transformed through the truth into a spiritual presence, a consciousness of mastery and dominion. The belief that one is mastered by adversity will be transformed into the realization that one is master himself and that all things are subordinate to him.

Confusion and sorrow give way to peace and joy when spiritual consciousness becomes active. The presence of spiritual truth in consciousness causes peace and joy to be omnipresent.

Paul fought a good fight and kept the faith. His loyalty to the cause strengthened his consciousness of the Lord as his deliverer and savior. If we are loyal to the truth, we can look to it to free and to deliver us.

The Lord will deliver me from every evil work,
and will save me unto his heavenly kingdom.

The presence of God is ever with me,
comforting and sustaining me at all times.

OCTOBER 14, 1927

When one feels alone or forsaken he may know that he does not know God; he does not realize that in Truth there is no lack or sorrow. One who knows God is free from all sense of loss, all feeling that he is forsaken or alone.

God is never apart or away from man. At the center of man's being, God abides. God is a wellspring of joy to all who find Him. He is a source of joy and comfort.

When those about you seem to make you unhappy, look to God. Turn within to Him; turn away from the person or the thing that seems to make you unhappy, and turn to the joy of Spirit. When you find God you will also find that no one can cause you discomfort. When you find God you will discover that those about you are working for your highest good. In the one who has seemed to cause you distress, you will find something of God.

When we find this rare, comforting presence we are able to help others to discover it. Having found God we can point the way to others who need His presence and His comfort.

We may be able to comfort them that are in any affliction,
through the comfort wherewith we ourselves are
comforted of God.—2 Corinthians 1:4

The saving and protecting power of God delivers me from every adverse situation and I am secure in Him.

MARCH 23, 1936

The presence of God within and about me is my protection. He ever saves and delivers me. I cannot run into any kind of danger, for He is ever with me as my protector. He is ever at hand to save me. My Savior is ever at hand, delivering me from adversity and causing me to know that I am secure in Him. He ever delivers me from the claims of evil, sin, fear, disease, failure, and death. He delivers me from every kind of adversity and causes me to feel that I am secure in Him.

Abiding in the consciousness of protection, I am ever protected. I cannot feel that I am apart or separated from Him. I cannot believe that I can be without His presence of protection, for He is ever with me. I rejoice to know that He is ever within and about me causing me to realize that He is right at hand at all times. I abide this day in the realization that the Spirit of God protects me. I live in the consciousness of protection. My Savior saves me. To Him I turn when I need protection.

He is able to save to the uttermost.—Hebrews 7:25

The spirit of God ever enfolds and protects me, and I go forth this day certain of its protection.

DECEMBER 27, 1936

The spirit of God is mighty to protect you from all harm. His spirit is the sanctuary of your salvation and protection. When you are conscious of His presence, you realize that He protects you from all danger. He is your deliverer from all sense of evil.

Do not go through life believing that things of the world can be a danger to you. Do not think of other persons as having power to harm you. Live in the consciousness that the spirit of God within and about you is mighty to save and protect you. If you will but get the clear realization of this, you will not need to give further thought to it.

You will get the consciousness of protection when you realize that in God's world there is no harm. When you lift your eyes to the vision of His world of good, you will see that danger cannot exist for you. You will find that the Spirit of God protects you first by clearing your mind of all belief in danger.

Under his wings shalt thou take refuge.—Psalm 91:4

*The enfolding presence of God's love
is my safety and protection.*

FEBRUARY 15, 1941

Because of his exalted vision Isaiah clearly perceived that God has been "a stronghold to the needy in his distress, a refuge from the storm." This not only was true in the past for those who sought God's help, but is true now, in this present day.

No matter from what we may seek protection, whether from inharmony, injustice, or hard circumstances, nothing can be so potent a salvation as the presence and power of God's love. To us it may seem that our difficulties can be solved only by some change in people or conditions. Aware of our inability to change them through our human strength, we tend to feel that we are entirely without protection.

Yet we are ever enfolded in divine protection. God is indeed our refuge when we realize that we can look to Him to adjust all things and to establish harmony in the midst of turmoil. The ever-present God is greater than any inharmony.

The Lord also will be a refuge ... in times of trouble.
—Psalm 9:9

> *I dwell in God, and I am conscious at all times of His protecting presence.*

MARCH 12, 1946

The realization that you live, move, and have your being in God brings to you a sense of peace and security. If you have been harboring thoughts of fear for yourself or for your loved ones, fear of storms, of accidents, of disease epidemics, release these thoughts now. Acknowledge that you and your dear ones abide eternally in the protecting presence of God.

Cultivate the habit of denying fear and affirm God's protecting presence in your daily life. Each morning place yourself and your dear ones in God's loving care and keeping, knowing that He will watch over you and keep you safe all through the day. Slippery roads, speeding motors, and all the seeming hazards of the material world bring no fear and uneasiness to the one whose faith is centered in God's abiding presence.

Put your whole trust in God, and He will keep you and yours safe and secure. He will watch over you and shield you and bring you safely through every experience. You will be conscious at all times of His protecting presence.

Be still, and know that I am God.—Psalm 46:10

From the Readers of Daily Word

I have received your Daily Word *for several months, and I would like to tell you that it is marvelous what it does for me. You know we young Germans saw a bit too much of hatred and despair during the war and it is hard for most of us to find the way back to a harmonious life. When I fled with my parents from East Germany in 1945 we did not know how life was to go on, having left everything behind us. Arriving in West Germany as refugees was harder than we had thought it would be. But finally things began to get better. My parents are wonderful. They took their total loss with almost a smile—but I was unhappy and inharmonious. Whatever I started did not seem to work out, and there seemed to be nothing but difficulties wherever I looked. Perhaps I tried too hard to get on.*

Now, I read Daily Word *several times a day. My situation has not changed very much, but I am losing this horrible tension in my thinking. I am now able to lay everything in the hands of God, and I am beginning to be happy and more harmonious.*

—FROM WEST GERMANY, NOVEMBER 1956

The presence of God watches over me;
wherever I am God is.

NOVEMBER 7, 1951

God, you are my protection, my blessing at all times. No matter where I am, I am not alone; for You are with me. Your presence watches over me now and every moment of the day and night.

You are not only around me and with me, but You are within me. I cannot stray beyond Your loving presence and tender care. Nor can my loved ones ever be separated from You.

I bless my dear ones, knowing that wherever they are You are with them. Your presence watches over them. You are with them to guide them, to bless them, to protect them.

If I seem to be alone with no human hand to steady me, no human heart to comfort me, I know that You are with me, God, steadying me, comforting me, strengthening me.

When I take a trip, I know that You go with me, making my way safe and happy.

I acknowledge Your presence and power as the only presence and power within me and about me. You are here, and I am safe and secure.

Here I am.—Isaiah 58:9

God is my protection. He blesses me at all times and under all circumstances.

AUGUST 10, 1958

The light of God surrounds me;
The love of God enfolds me;
The power of God protects me;
The presence of God watches over me.
Wherever I am, God is!
["Prayer for Protection," James Dillet Freeman]

"The light of God surrounds me." In His light there is no darkness; there is nothing to fear.

"The love of God enfolds me." God's love enfolds me and is like an armor around me; it is a comfort and assurance within me.

"The power of God protects me." His power protects me at all times and under all circumstances. He is my defense and my deliverance.

"The presence of God watches over me." I relax and trust His presence, which is within me, around me, at my right hand and at my left hand.

"Wherever I am, God is." Right where I am, God is. I cannot stray beyond His loving, protecting care. Wherever I go, God is.

And he led them safely, so that they feared not.
—Psalm 78:53

I am not alone, because the Father is with me.

OCTOBER 17, 1960

Jesus spoke these words of truth and we can speak them. We can speak them for ourselves; we can speak them for other persons. We are not alone, because the Father is with us. Circumstances may change, situations may be altered, the relationships we have known may no longer be a part of our experience. But we are not alone, because the Father is with us.

This truth never changes. It was true for Jesus. It has been and it will always be true for those persons who know their relationship to God. Knowing God as Father, knowing ourselves as His children, we understand His infinite love and compassion. We think of a natural father as caring for, protecting, comforting, sustaining his children. How much more then can God, who is the very principle of love and wisdom, be trusted to care for His children, to protect, comfort, and sustain them.

Yes, Jesus spoke these words, and we can speak them, for they are true.

I am not alone, because the Father is with me.—John 16:32

Thank you, God, for a new awareness of your protecting presence.

JANUARY 28, 1967

"Behold, I make all things new."

No matter what I have to meet, no matter how alone I may feel in some situation, always the presence of God is with me, always His help is at hand.

"I will fear no evil; for thou art with me." I think about these words from the 23rd Psalm, which have been a source of strength and help to many, many persons down through the years. When I know, truly know, that God is with me, then I am free from fear. I know that nothing in all the world can separate me from God. I move through every experience with a sense of freedom and security.

This realization of freedom from fear not only blesses me but blesses those persons who are a part of my life. I am not worried about the safety or well-being of another person when I know that God is with him at all times, in all places.

Yea, though I walk through the valley of the shadow of death, I will fear no evil: for thou art with me; thy rod and thy staff they comfort me.—Psalm 23:4

Beginning Again

Frank B. Whitney

It matters not what may befall;
Beyond all else, I hear the call:
"You can begin again."
My courage rises when I hear
God's voice allay the thought of fear
And when he whispers gently, near,
"You can begin again."

When once quite all the world
seemed wrong,
Throughout its din I heard his song:
"You can begin again."
And inner joy within me stirred,
I treasured each assuring word,

My heart was lifted when I heard:
"You can begin again."

Begin again? Another chance?
Can even I make an advance?
"You can begin again."
Begin at once by taking heart
And knowing God—of you he's part!
New life to you he will impart.
"You can begin again."

This edition of Daily Word *honored founder and editor Frank B. Whitney after his passing.*

Wherever I find myself, I acknowledge the protecting, guiding, sustaining presence of God.

MAY 29, 1970

When we travel or find ourselves away from the comfortable surroundings of home, we can know that God's presence is right there with us. We can carry a sense of security with us wherever we go. It is a matter of thinking about the protecting, guiding, sustaining presence of God.

We can establish ourselves in a feeling of protection by turning to God in prayer: "Father-God, I give thanks that Your presence is right here with me. Your light guides me; Your love sustains me; Your power protects me. I am in Your presence and all is well with me."

As we pray, we feel a closeness to God that overshadows any concern or worry. We see clearly the right steps to take. With inner confidence and assurance we go forth to meet our good.

No matter where we find ourselves, God is there with us.

In all your ways acknowledge him, and he will make straight your paths.—Proverbs 3:6

Hold thou my hand, be thou my guide.
My trust is in thee.

NOVEMBER 30, 1977

At morning's dawn, I feel Thy presence near. As sunlight filters through my window, so Thy light filters through my mind and transforms every dark thought into one of light. I am renewed and refreshed. In this light my life takes on new radiance and joy.

All through the hours of this day, I feel Thy presence close abiding. Thy loving Spirit upholds me. Thy presence enfolds me and gives me strength and support. In Thee I am strong. In Thee I am unafraid. In Thee I am upheld, sustained, and comforted.

In the night hours Thou art with me. I am enfolded in Thy presence. Thou art watching over me, protecting me, bringing me rest of body, mind, and spirit. The darkness is as light with Thee. Thy love casts out every shadow of fear.

Morning, noon, and night, dear Lord, I am holding Thy hand. My trust is in Thee.

Whither shall I go from thy Spirit? Or whither
shall I flee from thy presence?—Psalm 139:7

I fear no evil; for thou art with me.

FEBRUARY 7, 1981

There is nothing for me to fear, for God is with me at all times, in all places, and under all circumstances. God is protecting me, comforting me, guiding me, loving me, prospering me, and establishing me in perfect health.

I feel God's presence—loving, peaceful, healing, reassuring. I know that God is always ready to fulfill my every need. God's promise is, "Before they call I will answer, while they are yet speaking I will hear."

I put my faith in God and in His presence within me; therefore, I am not concerned with negative appearances or seeming lack and limitation. My absolute faith and trust in God show me the real, the lasting, the eternal good.

God's presence assures my safety. I fear no evil, no failure, no lack, no limitation. God is with me and I am secure.

I fear no evil.—Psalm 23:4

> *God's presence is a blessing of comfort and peace.*

APRIL 25, 1988

It is comforting to know that God is with me wherever I am, whatever I am doing. It helps me to keep on keeping on when I know that God is there to guide, strengthen, sustain, and protect me in every instant.

How much more comforting to know that God is *within* me as well as with me. I understand God's guidance as divine intelligence operating within me and through me. I feel God's strength within me as a quickening of pure life. I am sustained by divine power as energy moving through my very being. I feel God's protection as divine love radiating within me and through me, unifying me with the loving people around me.

I am comforted in knowing that the presence of God is *within* me, that the presence of God goes with me throughout every day and night.

Our soul waits for the Lord; he is our help and shield.
—Psalm 33:20

Wherever I am, God is.

APRIL 12, 1991

Wherever I go, whatever I do, the presence of God is with me. And wherever the presence of God is, there is unfailing love, understanding, and power for good.

Sometimes events or circumstances may suggest that I am somehow separated from the presence and power of God. However, I know that this is not so. If, for some reason, I do feel a lack of God's presence, I pause for a moment of prayer. In prayer, I turn to that sanctuary of God's presence within me, where I always find comfort and peace. As I rest in the realization of love, I am assured anew that God is protecting me wherever I am, wherever I go. I sense God's loving presence surrounding and enfolding me in a mantle of light.

Just as God's presence is always with me, it is also an ever-present reality in the lives of those I hold dear. I know that they are protected, and I am at peace.

In God, whose word I praise, in God I trust without a fear.—Psalm 56:4

God is my strength and my comfort.

MAY 24, 1997

There may be times in my life when I will need an extra measure of comfort and the reassurance of God's love in order to cope with the unexpected.

In these times, as in all times, God's strength enfolds and protects me in much the same way a cocoon protects a caterpillar as it transforms into a butterfly. I am enfolded by unconditional love that no person or situation can diminish. When the time is right and when I feel strong enough once again in mind and heart, I will emerge as a renewed creation of divine potential.

My comfort and strength come from God, the one source of the divine love and peace that create my reality. God is my strength and my comfort.

*You will have confidence, because there is hope;
you will be protected and take your rest in safety.—Job 11:18*

From the Readers of Daily Word

Daily Word *means a lot to me. It helps me to make each day and times of worry and fear.* Daily Word *gives me strength and a peaceful mind.*

— YVONNE H., CHICAGO

Daily Word *is nourishment for mind, body, and soul. I start my day with prayer and* Daily Word.

— EMMA H., RIVERDALE, GEORGIA

Daily Word *has always been so informative and enlightening about the true and never-changing word of God.*

— MARY B., WELDON, NORTH CAROLINA

Attuned to the wisdom and love of God,
I am secure in all circumstances.

APRIL 17, 2003

What blessed reassurance I feel in knowing that God's spirit is within me, within others, and in every particle of land, air, and sea. Wherever I am, God is with me and no matter where I may go, God accompanies me.

My relationship with God deepens each time I pray, each time I attune myself to the wisdom and love of my Creator. I feel secure and comfortable in new circumstances and while traveling in unfamiliar places.

I trust the spirit of God that is present in every circumstance, and I give thanks that wisdom and love are being expressed by me and others.

But let all who take refuge in you rejoice; let them ever sing for joy. Spread your protection over them, so that those who love your name may exult in you.—Psalm 5:11

367

God is all I need.

AUGUST 24, 2009

When we were children, we sometimes felt invincible. Nothing could stand in our way or harm us. Even if we did have a concern, we were quickly comforted by the embrace of a parent or other caring adult.

As adults, we may feel that those protective arms have fallen away. In such times of uncertainty, we can call on God's loving, sheltering presence.

The spirit of God is within us and goes before us. At any time, any one of us can "lean on the everlasting arms" and feel safe and secure.

We are children of God, always loved and supported.

For the promise is for you, for your children, and for all who are far away, everyone whom the Lord our God calls to him.—Acts 2:39

I am divinely protected in all ways.

MAY 27, 2010

What a comfort it is to know that I am always guided and supported by the presence of God, especially in times of change or challenge. There is only one Presence and one Power, God the good, omnipotent. Nothing and no one has power greater than this. Centered in this truth, I know that all is well.

Whatever I may be experiencing, I know that God is in me and God is also in the situation. Within me are the wisdom and strength I need to handle whatever circumstance may arise. Divine guidance and direction lead me through. No matter what the appearance, I am divinely protected in all ways.

When you walk through fire you shall not be burned ...
For I am the Lord your God.—Isaiah 43:2, 3

I am secure in God's loving presence.

APRIL 28, 2016

Being in my own home, where I am surrounded by my own things and the people and pets I love, gives me a sense of security. Yet anywhere I go, I can feel protected because I am secure in God's loving presence.

Although I cannot visibly see God's presence surrounding me, I know I am divinely protected. With God as my ever-present guide, I do not fear anything or anyone. I am serene and confident because God is with me. I am never alone. This awareness brings me true peace and comfort.

If I find myself facing a possibly dangerous situation, I remain calm. I have the strength and clarity of thought to recognize and accept what I need to do to stay safe. I am secure in God's loving presence.

But you, O Lord, are a shield around me, my glory, and the one who lifts up my head.—Psalm 3:3

Through my oneness with God, I feel protected.

AUGUST 8, 2021

Sometimes I may feel at the mercy of a changing, tumultuous world I cannot control. This is never true. Even though the chaos of the world may swirl around me, at the center of my being is a place of perfect peace and calm. Whenever I am in need of a safe refuge, I turn to God within to reach this place of tranquility and reclaim my feeling of security and protection.

The sun always rises after the longest, darkest night. I remind myself of this truth and feel grateful as I allow the light of spiritual understanding to release and reclaim whatever power I may have unwittingly given to a fear-based thought. Fully in tune with the divine presence within me, I move safely and confidently through every challenging circumstance.

The one who is in you is greater than the one who is in the world.—1 John 4:4

Messages of
JOY

Messages of JOY

Are joy and happiness different? In the Unity spiritual teachings, happiness is a response to circumstances, whereas joy is a state of being. We can experience joy no matter what is happening around us. Just as the apostle Paul said, "Give thanks in all things," we can feel joy in all things. We can bring joy and be joy wherever we are. Joy is part of our divine identity; it is our spiritual nature to dwell in joy. There may be dark times when joy seems hard to summon, but, like knowing the sun is shining behind the clouds, we can rest assured that joy is a part of our true essence.

The Response Is Tremendous

By J. Sig Paulson

NOVEMBER 1977

Praise and give thanks to God for the gift of eternal life within you, and you will find that the response is tremendous—electrifying, energizing, enduring! The kingdom (eternal life activity) of God is within us, and it is our heavenly Father's good pleasure to give us the kingdom. We, of course, as free souls, decide how we will respond to the free gift. We can wait for it, beg for it, work for it, scheme for it, go through all kinds of complicated rituals and practices for it—or we can joyously accept it with praise and thanksgiving.

Jesus Christ, who knew the Father of life so well, said He came that we might have life, and have it abundantly. He pointed out that the gift He came to bring would become, in the one who accepts it, a stream of living water (energy), welling up into eternal life. "For my gift will become a spring in the man himself, welling up into eternal life."

A little thought will clearly reveal that the religion of Jesus Christ is life. His gift to humanity is life, and His demonstration of victory over death is life—the only life there is, the eternal life of God. He revealed that eternal life is the creative, energetic, unfolding activity taking place in each individual as he accepts the free gift and becomes its awakening self-expression. It is not theory, speculation, or probability. It is the real thing—eternal life!

The abundant, healthy, loving, forgiving, freeing eternal life we all naturally desire is already within us, awaiting our acceptance, praise, and thanksgiving. Take my word for it only as an inspiration to prove it to yourself …

If you are willing, enter the activity outlined in the following statement: "I praise and give thanks to God for the gift of eternal life within me, and the response is tremendous—electrifying, energizing, enduring." Then be still a few moments and feel the response of life itself, our Creator, all creation, all humanity, yourself, including the atoms and cells of your body. Creator and creation rejoice as you accept the gift that is so freely given.

An awakening soul (yours) is joining the symphony of eternal life—and creation which has been "standing on tiptoe" waiting for this special event responds with glad shouts of thanksgiving that vibrate in your inner being, encouraging you to continue what you are doing.

Eternal life is contagious, irresistible, expanding in its operation in you. It is the work of the Holy Spirit, the activity of the whole Spirit of God. As you continue to accept it with praise and thanksgiving, your mind will be renewed and your whole being transformed by the energetic transfusion of radiant life.

There is a special, powerful, inexhaustible current of eternal life that is for you alone. It has your name on it! As you accept it, you will realize that it was there, within you, just waiting for you to wake up to its presence, power, and activity.

Praise your eternal life current, the gift of God in you. Rejoice in it! Love it! Appreciate it! Affirm its overcoming power! Joyously abandon old states of limitation, imitation, and frustration. Let life move you into new, creative, adventurous ways of self-expression, sharing, giving.

Joyously declare: "I praise and give thanks to God for the eternal life current that is constantly expanding its operation in my heart, soul, mind, body, and activities." Then relax in gratitude and let the expanding life current fill your mind and heart with new, lively, thoughts and feelings; your soul with new, lively revelations of truth; your body with new, lively energies; your relationships with new, lively dimensions; and your whole world with new, lively miracles of good.

You are being awakened by life itself, the activity of God. You will be delighted with a deepening sense of unity, of oneness with your Creator, and with all creation. Life unifies you with its source in you and in all creation. You become alive enough to know the truth that sets you free from all sense of separation. You are able to praise and give thanks for the eternal life current that makes you one with God, your neighbor, and the universe. And as all sense of separation is dissolved, you find it easy and natural to love the Lord your God with all your heart, soul, mind, and strength—and your neighbor as yourself.

Life is the activity of Infinite Love, the Creator of all, and as it expands its operation in you, love naturally wells up and flows in new, lively, and fulfilling ways. That is how the eternal life current operates in all who accept it …

With joyous praise and thanksgiving you will realize: "My life is the eternal, infinite life of God and the longer I live the more alive I am."

[J. Sig Paulson (1915–1998) traveled the world for Unity, served as minister of the Unity Village Chapel, then later was minister at Unity of Houston. A best-selling author, his articles and poems appeared in many Unity publications.]

Beloved Child

Norman V. Olsson

All that is innocent and pure
Within the child self will endure
And waits in the soul's deep recess
For precious moments to express.

O listen to that inner child,
God's own beloved, meek and mild.
God's ways so happy and carefree
Will lead us to simplicity!

I rejoice in the fullness of joy.

OCTOBER 31, 1924

Pray the true prayer of rejoicing and thanksgiving that All-Good is the only real thing in the universe.—Miscellaneous Writings

Our joy is commensurate with our consciousness that Good alone is real. When we know that adverse thought has no place, existence, or being in Truth, then is Good the only reality and the only presence to us. When we have subtracted all belief in evil and that which gives sadness, then alone is our world full of the very presence of God as our joy.

When one believes in two powers (good and evil) he recognizes that his joy may swing from one to the other. Be in instant prayer. Be in that strong consciousness of joy from which nothing can swerve you. Keep your thought true to the presence and the reality of good. Do not adulterate this presence by believing that anything can exist for you which is not good and joy-producing. Meet every situation through a strong consciousness of joy. Keep your joy established through often repeating declarations of joy.

"In thy presence is fullness of joy."

I am optimistic at all times because the joy of the Lord fills and thrills me.

JUNE 5, 1928

How easy it is for a person to cure himself of pessimism when he learns the truth about life! One does not find it hard to be an optimist when he views life from the standpoint of Truth.

The optimist has much in his favor. In the first place, he can rejoice because he is thinking according to God, the mighty principle of Truth. When one is filled with joy and good cheer he is letting himself be a channel through which the happy and sunny thoughts of God may be expressed.

Every situation in the life of an optimist must bring him good because his eyes behold good coming into manifestation regardless of appearances. How we change our world when we behold the manifestation of good in place of the appearance of evil!

The joy of the Lord fills us when we have emptied ourselves of the old thoughts of sadness, darkness, and pessimism. When we look upward we behold the sun of God shining upon us, revealing our good to us. When we gaze heavenward our vision seems to be cleared of negation and adversity and we become filled with optimism, joy, and heavenly benedictions.

That my joy may be in you, and that your joy may be made full.—John 15:11

The joy of the presence of Christ fills my heart,
and I am forever joyful.

OCTOBER 7, 1933

What greater joy can we have than the knowledge that Christ is within us, that He is the source of our joy, that He ever abides with us! Are we justified in ever being sad or sorrowful when we know this mighty truth? Can a sorrowful thought find place in our heart when we realize that the presence of joy abides there?

Are you joyful today? If not, you are probably thinking that other persons and external things have power to take your joy from you. You are believing that things of the world can make you unhappy. You are thinking that situations and circumstances produce joy and, all the while, the very presence of Christ in you is your constant source of joy.

In the presence of Christ there is bountiful joy. When we abide in this realization there can be naught but joy for us. When we realize that Christ is in us and we are in Him, nothing can take our joy from us. Nothing can make us sad or depressed. Realizing our oneness with joy, we cannot give any thought to the belief that things of the world can disturb us.

Then will I go unto the altar of God,
unto God my exceeding joy.—Psalm 43:4

The joy of God fills my heart,
and my whole being is filled with joy.

MARCH 14, 1937

When the joy of God fills us, there is no place for sorrow and depression. We cannot be sorrowful and at the same time rejoice in God. We cannot entertain thoughts of sadness when the joy of God fills our heart. We find that the joy of God causes us to rejoice in every situation.

Rejoice for every evidence of the goodness of God. Rejoice for the good that is coming to you this day. Rejoice for blessings visible and invisible. Let the Spirit of rejoicing so fill your heart that you no longer let sorrow dominate you. Let joy be your keynote today and view all situations through eyes of joy.

The joy of God is constant when it is enthroned in our heart. The things of the world cannot change or affect such joy. It is founded upon that which does not change or pass away. It has God for its foundation and substance. As a child of God you are entitled to great joy. Every experience in your life should contribute to your joy.

That my joy may be in you, and that your joy
may be made full.—John 15:11

I am inspired to ever-increasing joy.
I rejoice that Christ lives within me.

APRIL 15, 1941

The joy of Christ is what I seek, and it is this alone which can satisfy my inner need and desire. I may seek far and wide, but I fail to discover complete happiness, contentment, and satisfaction until I find Christ within myself as the joy of my life.

Turning from things of the outer to the quietness within, I find the Christ presence within me filling me with light and joy and radiance. Gladness floods my being, and my joy is increased. Nothing in the outer has power to make me sad or downcast. I know that Christ within me is the joy of my heart.

Many experiences in the life of Jesus Christ may appear to have been sad ones. But I know that He lived so close to the Father that joy and gladness filled His heart at all times. He rejoiced in living close to the Father. I too rejoice in following the life that He has shown to me.

Because Christ lives in me I daily dwell in His presence, and His eternal joy is mine.

Thou hast put gladness in my heart.—Psalm 4:7

In contemplation of thee, O Lord,
I find great joy and peace.

MAY 11, 1948

This moment which I have dedicated to Thee is blessed with Thy joy, and I find my heart filled with a feeling of peace and at rest in Thy love. As I commune with Thee I am renewed, my heart is filled with a song of joy, and my soul is flooded with light.

In any time of bewilderment I turn to Thee. My chaotic thoughts find their orderly pattern, and the hurried beating of my heart finds a quieter rhythm. I go forward with purpose and with courage, my soul shielded in deep faith.

In prayer I find my fears vanquished, my sorrow transformed, my faith increased and strengthened.

Feelings of futility are conquered by Thy joy within me. The terror of fear fades into nothingness before Thy eternal light. Sorrow becomes but a shadow. Joy and peace reign in my heart and soul.

I am at peace in Thee.

Everlasting joy shall be upon their heads:
they shall obtain gladness and joy, and sorrow
and sighing shall flee away.—Isaiah 35:10

From the Readers of Daily Word

Daily Word *has been a blessing to me for more than 45 years. I love reading and receiving courage daily, and the prayer line has given me strength in hard times.*

—J.S., POPLAR BLUFF, MISSOURI

I enjoy reading each day's message, as I have for years. Helps me to focus for the day on what really matters. It's my morning meditation!

—M.P., LITTLE ROCK, ARKANSAS

My good friend gave me my first subscription to Daily Word *in 1999 when I was going through a difficult time. I have renewed my subscription ever since. I never miss a day reading it. It has been a lifesaver and has strengthened my faith.*

—D.B.

I stir up the spirit of joy that God has implanted in my heart.

MARCH 30, 1951

Many persons, without realizing it, wear a glum, unhappy expression. They are not really unhappy, but they are preoccupied with their own thoughts and problems and do not express a joyful spirit.

Just as in Truth we learn to watch our thoughts and our words, we can learn to watch our facial expressions. We can cultivate a look of serenity, of joy, of goodwill.

We do not need to wait for something to happen in order to express joy. We have a spirit of joy within us that can be stirred into expression at any time.

To be joyful is a natural state for us as children of God; in fact it is more natural for us to be joyful than to be gloomy. The more we let the spirit of joy that God has implanted in our heart find expression through us the greater is our capacity for enjoyment and appreciation of life.

Let us stir up the spirit of joy that God has implanted in our heart.

For ye shall go out with joy, and be led forth with peace.
—Isaiah 55:12

I live; I love; I laugh; I enjoy life.

NOVEMBER 10, 1958

The joy of the Lord is my strength. I let the joy of the Lord bubble up within me and overflow into my thoughts, words, and actions. I remember that it is the Father's good pleasure to give me the strength of His joy.

I live; I love; I laugh; I enjoy life.

I will not take myself or my problems too seriously. I know that the Spirit of God within me is fully capable of seeing me through this day's experiences joyously and successfully. So I turn the direction of my life over to God. He guides my way and lifts any burdens from my shoulders. Because I am open and responsive to His Spirit I find myself blessed with a new sense of joy and strength.

I live; I love; I laugh; I enjoy life.

The joy of the Lord floods over me, and my faith is strong. I know that God is at work. I live as God created all men to live, joyously, fully, confidently, and splendidly. I am a radiating center of the joy of the Lord, mighty to radiate good to others and to attract my own good.

The joy of Jehovah is your strength.—Nehemiah 8:10

I am filled with joy. I express joy.

MARCH 29, 1960

It is impossible for me to speak the prayer for today with meaning and feeling and keep the corners of my mouth turned downward.

What a beauty treatment joy is! When there is joy in the heart there is an uplift of the spirit that uplifts the face and form. When there is joy in the heart there is a smile on the lips and a light in the eyes.

"I am filled with joy." As I speak this part of the statement I may want to count my blessings. I may want to take stock of the joys that fill my life. Giving thought to joy helps me to release any thought that has clouded my mind and shadowed my expression.

"I express joy." Do I? Do I look and act and speak as a joyous person does? If I find it difficult to feel and express my joy, it is time for me to stir myself to a new and deeper sense of appreciation. It is time for me to recognize myself as a son of God. It is time for me to let that naturally joyous son of God shine through.

And my mouth shall praise thee with joyful lips.
—Psalm 63:5

Thank you, Father, for a song of joy in my heart today.

FEBRUARY 17, 1968

Thank you, Father, for a song in my heart today. I listen in the inner stillness for Your song of life and love within me. No matter what my problem, grief, or fear, I now let go and feel Your blessing. I receive the help I need to overcome anything.

I relax. I am at peace. I am still. I enter into Your harmony and love, Father. I listen to Your song of joy. My heart beats in unison with Your great heart of love. Deep within me I feel my oneness with You.

All the static of outer disturbance dissolves as Your quietness and peace pervade my being. Deep within me I listen. I hear the melody of love that is within me and all around me. I hear it now. I keep my inner ear listening as I go about my daily tasks. Thank You, Father, for Your melody of love and joy that sings within me. My heart is happy. Thank You, Father, for a song in my heart today.

So he led forth his people with joy, his chosen ones with singing.—Psalm 105:43

The Croaker

The Oklahoma Mason

Once on the edge of a pleasant pool,
Under the bank where 'twas dark and cool,
Where bushes over the water hung,
And rushes nodded and grasses swung,
Just where the crick flowed outer the fog,
There lived a grumpy and mean old frog,
Who'd sit all day in the mud and soak
And just do nothing but croak an' croak,
Till a blackbird hollered, "I say, yer know,
What's the matter down there below?
Are you in trouble, er pain, er what?"
The frog sez, "Mine is an orful lot;
Nothing but mud and dirt and slime
For me to look at just all the time.
It's a dirty world!" so the old fool spoke,
"Croakity croakity croakity croak!"

"But yer looking down!" the blackbird said;
"Look at the blossoms overhead,
Look at the lovely summer skies,
Look at the bees and butterflies,
Look up, old feller. Why, bless your soul,
Yet looking down in a muskrat hole!"
But still with a gurgling sob and choke
The blamed ole critter would only croak,
And a wise old turtle, who boarded near,
Sez to the blackbird, "Friend, see here:
Don't shed no tears over him, fer he
Is low-down just 'cause he likes ter be;
He's one er them kind of chumps that's glad
To be so mis-rable-like and sad;
I'll tell yer something that ain't no joke,
Don't waste yer sorrer on folks that croak."

The joy of the Lord is my strength.

JANUARY 10, 1971

Are you faced with a situation that seems utterly devoid of joy? Here is an idea that can change this situation and change your thought about it. Even though you cannot see how joy can possibly be injected into it, as you think about the situation say to yourself, "The joy of the Lord is my strength." Repeat these words until the thought of joy begins to take hold in your consciousness. Note that you are saying, "The joy of the Lord is my strength." We find joy in many things, but the true source of all joy—joy in life, joy in work, joy in our hearts—is the joy of the Lord, the joy that is deep within our souls.

The Father created you to be joyful; He blesses you with the strength of joy.

It may take persistence to maintain a spirit of joy. The mountain climber approaches his task with joy. He does not quail or falter, however steep or treacherous the ascent. And the joy he feels as he works his way upward is his strength. You, too, can conquer your mountain as you let the joy of the Lord well up within you.

Enter thou into the joy of thy Lord.—Matthew 25:21

I greet this day with joy. I put joy into each activity of this day.

JUNE 18, 1976

Some people spend their time thinking of the past or looking to the future, and never truly enjoy the present moment. A wise person said, "He who like a little child lives adventurously from moment to moment, day to day, experiencing the spontaneous joy of life, is the one who truly knows happiness." Perhaps we need to remind ourselves that life is a joyous adventure, that to regard it in any other way is to miss its blessing.

We were meant for joy and happiness; we are joyous by nature. Joy does not depend upon any person, condition, or thing. Joy is within us, and we can tap this great reservoir of joy by turning within and becoming aware of the presence of God within us. God is our source of joy. Our part is to let God's Spirit of joy express itself through us. No matter what our present need or problems, we can put joy into each activity of this day.

For you shall go out in joy, and be led forth in peace.
—Isaiah 55:12

God's joy upholds, blesses,
and strengthens me all day long.

JULY 16, 1993

Even during familiar routines, I want to experience and reflect joy. And I can, for joy is my soul's true inheritance. As I let joy pervade my thoughts and attitudes, it expresses itself in many ways.

God's joy wells up within me as an unquenchable, bubbling spring of gladness. Joy is my strength, my stronghold in times of stress and strain. The joy of God upholds me continually.

I take joy with me wherever I go. I am cheerful at home, work, and all points in between. I communicate joy to everyone.

God's joy is awaiting my recognition. I let it permeate my mind and heart and affirm that nothing can stop its flow. Joy circulates into all areas of my life, blessing me and everyone I associate with. My world is brightened with joy.

Thou hast put more joy in my heart.—Psalm 4:7

God has created me in joy
and created me to express joy.

MARCH 21, 1997

I may feel no joy in being caught in rush-hour traffic. But if I happen to turn on the car radio and hear a resounding chorus of Beethoven's "Ode to Joy," I can't help but be filled with feelings of gladness.

What has happened? The joy of one of the world's greatest composers has reached across more than a century of time to strike a chord of joy within me.

Once the traffic begins to move, I feel lighthearted and in no need to hurry. So I let the driver next to me change lanes and get in front of me. Yes, I am being the joy of God I was created to be.

The joy that God created Beethoven to express is the same joy I was created to express also. I may not compose a work of art, but a simple act of kindness can sound a note of joy within others.

And the disciples were filled with joy
and with the Holy Spirit.—Acts 13:52

From the Readers of *Daily Word*

A friend sent me Daily Word *many years ago and I have continued to subscribe and also send to friends. I have been blessed by reading and practicing these thoughts—very uplifting for me.*

—B.S., PALESTINE, TEXAS

It always helps my day no matter what.

—C.T., PITTSBURGH, PENNSYLVANIA

My husband and I read the Daily Word *every evening before dinner. It always brings a positive spin to whatever events happened throughout the day! It also gives a great start to our dinner conversation as many of the devotions we read could be connected to past events. It is great!*

—D.W., SEWELL, NEW JERSEY

The spirit of God fills me with joy,
and I express the joy of living!

FEBRUARY 24, 2000

My experiences of joy vary. For instance, the sudden burst of laughter is a moment of gladness. However, the underlying joy I feel from just being alive with the life of God is constant.

This is the joy of Spirit that encourages me to turn even the most mundane tasks into a pleasant experience. Divine joy is such an integral part of who I am that it is naturally reflected in all that I do and say.

Whether I am cleaning my closets or walking my dog, I do so with joy in my soul and a lightness of spirit. The reward of a joyful soul is a deep satisfaction in doing a job and in doing it well.

The spirit of God fills me with joy—and I express the joy of living!

Let us come into his presence with thanksgiving; let us make
a joyful noise to him with songs of praise!—Psalm 95:2

I know and express joy,
unlimited and full of gratitude.

JANUARY 16, 2009

In our humanness, there are physical activities, events, and accomplishments that bring us joy. From our subtle giggles and chuckles with friends to our cheering shouts in a crowd, we unite in expressions of happiness. We exchange the jubilance of the human spirit with abilities to inspire one another, to thrive individually, and to expand joyfully amidst a multitude of life's happenings.

The joy of the Spirit is the greatest joy because it is pure, deep, and powerful. In any moment—whether still or exuberant, happy or serious—we can experience the joy of Spirit. Allowing ourselves to acknowledge that God's spirit is within us, enfolding us, we know and express joy, unlimited and full of gratitude.

I have indeed received much joy and encouragement from your love, because the hearts of the saints have been refreshed through you, my brother.—Philemon 1:7

I am thrilled with the joy of living.

NOVEMBER 8, 2011

Have I been merely existing rather than knowing the full joy of living? To experience the transformative power of joy, I let the Christ Spirit move in me. I act from Christ consciousness and allow it to inform my thoughts, lighten and lift my vision, and create about me an atmosphere of peace and happiness.

Joy is a result of interest and awareness, of active appreciation and creative expression. I take time to be interested in my neighbor's welfare and offer a helping hand. I see the beauty of nature and hear music in the hum of the day's activities. I recognize the Christ in myself and in others. I let my soul be thrilled and exalted as I actively and purposefully take joy in living a full and complete life.

With joy you will draw water from the wells of salvation.
—Isaiah 12:3

I infuse laughter, dance, and song into my day.

JUNE 17, 2016

It's easy to get caught up in the seriousness of life, so I make a point of doing things that bring joy. I become a natural conduit of happiness for others when I remember that joy is my natural state of being.

Life is intended to be joyful. It's easy for me to focus on everyday tasks or the seriousness of worldly news, yet I am not here on this earth to be somber. I am a messenger of joy, and the joy of Spirit is moving through me.

I feel free and light as I express joy without censor. Today I free myself to do things that bring me joy. As I express myself in these ways, I also become a conduit of joy for those around me. My joy is contagious! I give thanks to God for joy—this natural state of being. I commit to living in joy every day.

Be glad in the Lord and rejoice, O righteous, and shout for joy, all you upright in heart.—Psalm 32:11

Divine joy is mine.

OCTOBER 15, 2020

Joy is a natural part of my identity, the song my heart sings. I live my life from the depth of joy that comes from God and is part of my divine identity. As joy fills my entire body, my heart overflows with peace and well-being. If I am not feeling joyful, I know I can connect with joy again and again because joy is a constant state of being, always mine to claim for myself.

To feel joy deep in my heart, I prepare myself to receive it. Prayer, meditation, and a gratitude practice open me to receive the infinite supply of God. I remember people, places, and experiences that fill me with delight, and as I do I feel joy fill me like water drawn from a well. I keep the feeling alive by recalling favorite memories, slowing down to notice the beauty in a flower or sunset, or hearing the laughter of people having fun. Every time I seek joy, I find it.

And my spirit rejoices in God my Savior.—Luke 1:47

A Final Word

Readers who know and love *Daily Word* probably cannot picture a world without it, nor can we at Unity. People will always need spiritual support, spiritual tools and practices, and an understanding of their own spiritual nature.

What we can't predict is exactly the form *Daily Word* will take over the next 100 years. After its first century, *Daily Word* is still primarily a print publication. Only about 10 percent of the subscriptions are for the digital version delivered by email every day. *Daily Word* is also available to read with an app or on the *unity.org* website for those who have a subscription, accompanied by an audio recording of each day's message. It is translated into braille and audio CDs for those who are visually impaired.

But who knows what new technologies lie in store? Charles Fillmore, Unity cofounder, was an early adopter of telephone and radio and was fascinated by new inventions and scientific discoveries in the early 20th century.

"You can rest assured we will continue to innovate and modernize how we offer *Daily Word*," said Angie Olson, vice president of digital marketing and strategy for Unity World Headquarters. "Our goal is to make this timeless resource available to readers around the world using the technologies they become most familiar with in the next 100 years."

Added Unity CEO Jim Blake: "Other areas being explored are messaging for specific audiences and additional companion products to assist in one's spiritual journey."

What never changes is our oneness with God and our need to remember every day that we are divine beings in a human experience. We affirm that *Daily Word* will always be available to remind us of that Truth.